W9-AJS-646

Butterfly McQueen Remembered

Stephen Bourne

THE SCARECROW PRESS, INC.
Lanham, Maryland • Toronto • Plymouth, UK
2008

SCARECROW PRESS, INC.

Published in the United States of America
by Scarecrow Press, Inc.
A wholly owned subsidary of
The Rowman & Littlefield Publishing Group, Inc.
4501 Forbes Boulevard, Suite 200, Lanham, Maryland 20706
www.scarecrowpress.com

Estover Road
Plymouth PL6 7PY
United Kingdom

British Library Cataloguing in Publication Information Available

Library of Congress Cataloging-in-Publication Data

Bourne, Stephen, 1957–
  Butterfly McQueen remembered / Stephen Bourne.
    p. cm.
  Includes bibliographical references and index.
  ISBN-13: 978-0-8108-6018-6 (pbk. : alk. paper)
  ISBN-10: 0-8108-6018-X (pbk. : alk. paper)
  1. McQueen, Butterfly. 2. Motion picture actors and actresses—United States—
Biography. I. Title.

PN2287.M5468B68 2008
791.4302'8092—dc22
[B]

                              2007022323

∞™ The paper used in this publication meets the minimum requirements of American
National Standard for Information Sciences—Permanence of Paper for Printed Library
Materials, ANSI/NISO Z39.48-1992.
Manufactured in the United States of America.

~

Contents

~

Foreword

In 1952 I was hanging out with a group of friends who were interested in theatre. Two of them, Frank and Kevin, said, "Butterfly McQueen is holding auditions for a show on Saturday. How would you like to come along?" I wasn't interested in acting at that time. I was doing my college work, my undergraduate degree, and working full time, but I agreed to go along, just to watch Frank and Kevin. Butterfly had rented some space at the Carnegie Recital Hall for the auditions, and about eight of us showed up, which was quite a large group. Guys and girls. Black and white. We were integrated and brought together by our interest in theatre. She was delighted by the invasion. She told us all to sit down. She had copies of William Shakespeare's A Midsummer Night's Dream and, referring to me, she said I might read Demetrius or Lysander, and I just went along with it. Instantly I saw that this woman, whom I only knew as Prissy in Gone With the Wind, was superior to any of the roles she played in Hollywood because as various people started to read the lines, she would correct them, not rudely, but it was enough to discourage some of them from coming back, because she was going to make sure they sounded the way Shakespeare should. I was amazed at the depth and breadth of her knowledge. That was just awesome.

So the night ended and she took names, addresses, and phone numbers. She didn't call back some of the others, but she did call me, and I went back. On this occasion she had rented the Carnegie Recital Hall on a Sunday evening, just to accommodate me because I'd told her I couldn't make it on the

Saturday. I was impressed! She told me so much about the use of my voice, how to breathe. I got some intensive tutoring.

Her vision was to stage *A Midsummer Night's Dream* with people of color and she wanted to bring music to it, Latin music, and she was thinking of samba or rumba. She had her own personal vision of the play, which would be different, but there was no real possibility for her to produce Shakespeare with a black cast in America at that time. I believe she was living out a dream. But perhaps there were places where she could have done this. She could have brought it to the Apollo Theatre in Harlem, or the American Negro Theatre. She had the connections, but she needed the funding, and the image of Prissy would have been a plus and a minus. She could get in to explain the ideas, because who didn't know Prissy in *Gone With the Wind*? But then, once she was in, they would say, "Why aren't you gonna do a farce or an Amos and Andy type of thing?" It must have been difficult for her to cope emotionally with this, but I saw her as a person who was always with enough initiative to redirect her life. If a door closed, she would find another door to open.

Way after this encounter with me she got her college degree. She went to City College in Harlem in New York. It's a major college where you don't have to be wealthy to get a degree. And Butterfly lived in Harlem then, within walking distance of the college. By then I had become dean of faculty at the Borough of Manhattan Community College, and I was delighted when I heard that she had graduated with a bachelor of arts degree. This would have been in 1975. Three years later I saw her one-woman show at Reno Sweeney's. Afterwards I didn't go backstage to see her, but now I wish I had.

At my college I had an author on my faculty, his name was Roger Dooley, and in 1981 he published his book *From Scarface to Scarlett: American Films in the 1930s*. As dean I was expected to create events, so I had a reception at the Spanish Institute on Park Avenue for Roger, to help promote his book, and I thought of Butterfly McQueen. She had a bachelor of arts degree, she was connected to the college, so I invited her. Other actors who were around in the 1930s were also invited, including Joan Bennett and Walter Abel, and Butterfly showed up! Nearly thirty years had passed since we last met, and she didn't remember me. So I went up to her, and reminded her about the reading for *A Midsummer Night's Dream*, and I said: "I know that you have a copy of my book dedicated to you [*Blacks in American Films*] because I made sure that it was sent to you," and she was just so happy about it. And I said: "It was appropriate that you came here tonight because Mr. Dooley's book is about American films in the 1930s and 1940s and you were part of that." And she was just so delighted, and I was happy that I had invited her.

When Butterfly worked in Hollywood movies, she did her own thing with those silly maid parts. In those situations, actresses like Butterfly just did what it took to survive. In *Mildred Pierce*, when she answers the phone, the character she plays doesn't know one end of the phone from the other. Butterfly was paid to play a silly maid, but she did her own thing, and did it just beautifully. She was also memorable as Vashti in that scene with Lillian Gish in *Duel in the Sun*. She asks her mistress if there is anyone on the ranch she can marry. But the ranch is in the middle of nowhere! She never put down *Gone With the Wind* and always spoke highly of Clark Gable, Vivien Leigh, and David O. Selznick. She was such a great human being. But it's a pity that, when Butterfly was alive, we didn't do archival work the way we do it these days. There would have been so much to ask this woman on the subject of black women in films.

—Edward Mapp

In 1972 Edward Mapp dedicated his first book to Butterfly—Blacks in American Films: Today and Yesterday (see introduction). He was interviewed about Butterfly McQueen for this foreword by Stephen Bourne in London on August 9, 2006.

~

Acknowledgments

I would like to thank the following for their help and friendship: Christopher S. Connelly, James Gavin, Keith Howes, Delilah Jackson, Professor Edward Mapp, Deborah Montgomerie, Robin Mukerji, Tim Reid (The Autograph Collector), David Richardson, Ken Sephton, and Aaron Smith.

Special thanks go to Donald Bogle for his invaluable work on African American cinema, and to Charles Stumpf for "Remembering Butterfly McQueen," published in *Films of the Golden Age* in 1996 (see bibliography).

Acknowledgment is due to the late Butterfly McQueen for giving me permission to publish her "writings" (see appendix C). Butterfly distributed copies of these "essays" and "booklets" of personal comments and observations at appearances she made in the 1970s and 1980s. Copies were sent to the author with a letter, dated September 29, 1982, giving permission to publish them.

All the photographs in this book come from the author's private collection except the portrait by Albert Leonard and the photograph by Geraint Lewis, which have been reproduced with their permission.

I would also like to thank the New York Public Library, particularly the Schomburg Center for Research in Black Culture and the Library for the Performing Arts at Lincoln Center; the British Film Institute; and the British Library.

Though every care has been taken, if we have included any copyright material without acknowledgment or permission, through inadvertence or failure to trace the present owners, we offer our apologies to all concerned.

This book is dedicated to the film historian Donald Bogle, and to the memory of the other African American actors who appeared in *Gone With the Wind*: Eddie "Rochester" Anderson (Uncle Peter) (1905–1977); Everett Brown (Big Sam) (1902–1953); Daisy Bufford (Housemaid—evening prayers) (1913–1987); Ben Carter (Jeems) (1911–1946) (performance deleted); William McClain (Old Levi) (1863–1944); Hattie McDaniel (Mammy) (1895–1952); Oscar Polk (Pork) (1899–1949); Blue Washington (Renegade's companion) (1898–1970); Ernest Whitman (Carpetbagger's Friend) (1893–1954); and Zack Williams (Elijah) (1884–1958).

~

Introduction

When I signed the contract for this book on May 20, 2006, Butterfly Mc-
Queen had been lost to us for just over ten years. Her participation in *Gone
With the Wind*, arguably the most famous film ever made, needed to be docu-
mented. For decades, in the many books that have been published about
Gone With the Wind, the authors have either ignored, undervalued, or mis-
represented her. Biographies have been published about the film's producer,
David O. Selznick, and its main stars, Clark Gable and Vivien Leigh. Two
biographies have been published about the African American actress Hattie
McDaniel, famous for her Oscar-winning portrayal of Mammy in the film.
It is my personal view that Butterfly has been treated very badly. However,
there have been exceptions. Since the 1970s, the African American film
historian Donald Bogle has raised Butterfly's profile, and Charles Stumpf's
appraisal of her life and career in the fan magazine *Films of the Golden Age* in
1996 offers fascinating insights into the personal and professional struggles of
the actress. With the seventieth anniversary of the release of *Gone With the
Wind* approaching on December 15, 2009, and the centenary of Butterfly's
birth on January 8, 2011, I feel strongly that she has to have a book written
about her. I hope I can do justice to this great lady in the pages that follow.

I first heard about *Gone With the Wind* from my mother. When I was a child
in the 1960s she occasionally mentioned it, perhaps when Max Steiner's famous "Tara's Theme" was being played on the radio, or when she heard that
the star of the film, Vivien Leigh, passed away in 1967. When my mother
spoke about *Gone With the Wind*, she conjured up an image in my mind of a

special movie, different from the Walt Disney "family" films we saw at our local cinema, Peckham Odeon, in southeast London. For my mother, seeing the film at the age of eleven with Aunt Esther in 1942 at the Fulham Forum in west London was an important event in her young life. The Civil War epic swept her away when she first saw it. The world was experiencing a real war then, and air-raid-weary Londoners, like my mother and Aunt Esther, were forever seeking entertainment and escapism. *Gone With the Wind* provided this, and my mother *always* remarked upon the extraordinary length of the film. It was nearly four hours long, but she pointed out that there *was* an intermission, referred to as a "tea break," which lasted about fifteen minutes. However, in spite of the film's extraordinary length, unprecedented for a film at that time, she said the romance of its leading characters, Scarlett O'Hara and Rhett Butler, held the audience spellbound.

Aunt Esther also loved the film and spoke about it with fondness. A working-class black Londoner, she was a young woman of twenty-nine when she took my mother to see it. When I enquired about the film, she remarked upon Vivien Leigh's impressive performance as the film's strong-willed, feisty heroine Scarlett, and she saw nothing offensive about its stereotypical black characters, Mammy and Butterfly's character, Prissy. As far as Aunt Esther was concerned, bossy, cantankerous, but lovable Mammy and chirpy but simple-minded Prissy were part of the spectacular—but fictitious—world created in the movie by its producer, David O. Selznick, from Margaret Mitchell's best-selling novel. In spite of its romanticized view of slavery in America's "Old South," Aunt Esther welcomed four hours of "escapism" from Blitz-torn London.

Aunt Esther knew about slavery. Her father had told her she was the granddaughter of slaves in Guyana, a former colony known as British Guiana, when it was part of the British Empire. They were treated no better than those on the plantations in America's Deep South, and this saddened her. However, her father instilled in his daughter a sense of black pride, especially in those black heroes who existed when she was born in Edwardian England, such as the composer Samuel Coleridge-Taylor and the world-famous boxing champion Jack Johnson. Her father also took her to see many famous music hall (vaudeville) stars of the day, including G. H. Elliott, the blackface entertainer popularly known as "the chocolate coloured coon." Aunt Esther did not take offence at G. H. Elliott or a movie stereotype like Prissy because she was able to distinguish between reality and theatrical figures who provided entertainment and escapism. However, unlike Prissy, she would make a stand against anyone who disrespected or racially abused her. If Scarlett O'Hara had slapped her, my aunt would have slapped her back![1]

In 1970, at the age of twelve, with a little bit of money I had managed to save, I purchased my first two film books at the Cinema Bookshop situated in Great Russell Street off Tottenham Court Road. The books were David Shipman's *The Great Movie Stars: The Golden Years* and Lawrence J. Quirk's *The Films of Joan Crawford*. The cover of Shipman's book featured Vivien Leigh and Clark Gable as Scarlett and Rhett, and inside he profiled all four stars of the film: the other two were Olivia de Havilland (as Melanie) and Leslie Howard (as Ashley). This is where I began to learn more about the importance of the film. In *The Films of Joan Crawford*, there was a section about *Mildred Pierce* (1945), the melodrama for which Crawford won the Best Actress Oscar. A photograph used to illustrate the film features a light-hearted scene in the kitchen of Mildred's restaurant with Mildred (Crawford) tying a white apron around her friend Wally Fay (Jack Carson). In the background stands a black woman who is smiling at the couple, but the caption does not identify the actress who is playing her. Only Jack Carson's name is mentioned. I recognized the actress as the same one who had played Ethel Waters's friend, Lily, in *Cabin in the Sky* (1943), which I had seen for the first time on television in 1968. When I eventually saw *Gone With the Wind*, I realized that the unidentified actress in the photograph from *Mildred Pierce* was also the same actress who portrayed the hysterical servant girl Prissy in the Civil War epic. Butterfly McQueen was her name. Later, when I saw *Mildred Pierce* on television, I realized that Miss McQueen had a small but memorable role, but I was disappointed that she was not identified by Lawrence J. Quirk in *The Films of Joan Crawford*, and this worried me. In time, the world of Butterfly McQueen would open up to me, and I would understand—though not necessarily approve of—why such oversights occurred.

I first saw *Gone With the Wind* during its 1971 reissue. I was just thirteen, and still a schoolboy, but I had already started excusing myself from school in the afternoons—without permission—and taking myself off to the cinema. I was so desperate to see *Gone With the Wind* that I traveled into London's West End, instead of waiting for the film to come locally to Peckham Odeon. On arriving at the cinema in Haymarket, near Piccadilly Circus, I discovered a *very* long queue. I wasn't the only one who was missing school—or work—to see this popular film. By the time I bought my ticket and entered the auditorium, it was packed, and the only seat available to me was in the front row. My first viewing of *Gone With the Wind* was made difficult because the big screen—which was right in front of me—was overwhelming and almost impossible to look at for nearly four hours. A few weeks later I saw *Gone With the Wind* again in more comfortable circumstances when the film was distributed to local cinemas. Excusing myself from school again, I took myself off to Peckham Odeon, and this time I made sure I sat in the back row, which gave me a full view of the screen! From then on I took every opportunity to see the film, which was difficult because, in the 1970s, we had no access to video or DVD releases. They hadn't been invented! *Gone With the Wind* did not receive its British television premiere until the BBC screened it—with much fanfare—in two parts over Christmas 1981.

The film impressed me in the same way it had impressed my mother and Aunt Esther. It is a grandiose spectacle, full of melodrama, romance, gorgeous Technicolor, and memorable performances. The spectacular burning-of-Atlanta sequence is thrilling. The moment when the camera pulls back to reveal Scarlett walking among hundreds of dead and wounded soldiers is shocking, and breathtaking. After Scarlett returns home to a war-battered Tara, she makes an emotionally charged speech about never going hungry again—just before the intermission. It always moves me to tears. Scarlett O'Hara and Rhett Butler *are* the screen's greatest lovers; after all, Miss Leigh is extremely beautiful, and Mr. Gable is very sexy. The two stars bring the romantic entanglement of the two characters brilliantly to life. However, when I first saw the film, it was Butterfly McQueen in the small but memorable role of the hysterical, fragile servant girl, Prissy, who made the biggest impression, though Hattie McDaniel came close, as Scarlett's outspoken, feisty Mammy (see chapter 4). I had read everything I could about the film and its legendary quartet of stars: Leigh, Gable, de Havilland, and Howard, but I could find nothing about Butterfly. It was as if she only existed inside that film. I knew this wasn't the case, because I had seen her in *Cabin in the Sky* and in the photograph from *Mildred Pierce* in my Joan Crawford book. Happily, I did not have to wait long to discover who Butterfly was, what else she did in Hollywood, and what happened to her.

The turning point for me was reading Donald Bogle's book *Toms, Coons, Mulattoes, Mammies and Bucks: An Interpretive History of Blacks in American Films* (see chapter 3). I discovered this in the Cinema Bookshop in 1974. By that time I had seen Butterfly in at least two more movies: *Mildred Pierce* and *Duel in the Sun*. Mr. Bogle's critical appraisal of the work of black actors in Hollywood cinema opened the door for me. He described how Hollywood films had perpetuated racial stereotypes for decades, and highlighted the difficulties faced by actors and actresses like Butterfly who were unable to shake off the stereotypical images they had helped to create. Mr. Bogle also described Butterfly's performance in *Gone With the Wind* as one that is "marked by fragility, hysteria, and absurdity . . . a unique combination of the comic and the pathetic."[2] On reading this, I immediately made a connection with Mr. Bogle's assessment of Butterfly's characterization. It confirmed what I had suspected, that Butterfly was a gifted but misunderstood actress who, under impossible circumstances, humanized a racial caricature in one of the world's most famous films. In the introduction to his book, Bogle recalled an experience he described as "traumatic" when, in Chicago in 1969, he was working as a young staff writer for *Ebony*, America's top-selling black magazine:

> Having recently seen the reissued *Gone With the Wind*, I suggested to the managing editors of the magazine that we do a feature story on Butterfly McQueen, who portrayed Prissy. There was a renewed interest in her career because of the film and also her comeback on the stage in *Curley McDimple*. She was a nostalgic favorite for older readers, I assumed, and I had hoped that an article on McQueen might serve as a kick-off for a series on other forgotten black performers. To my surprise, I heard the *Ebony* editors sounding off like my former grade-school classmates. They dismissed the old-time actors as toms and mammies and spoke of them with boredom, disgust, contempt, and even condescension—as if our bright new movies of the 1960s with their bright new black actors had arrived at something called cinematic integrity! The attitude of the *Ebony* editors, however, simply pointed out the sad state of black film history in America. There was no history. And it seemed to me that a number of talented people were dismissed or ignored or even vilified because no one knew anything about the nature of their work and the conditions under which they performed. No, I thought. The past had to be contended with. It had to be defined, recorded, reasoned with, and interpreted. And I felt it was my task to do so.[3]

I wanted to see Butterfly in more films, but through further research at the British Film Institute I discovered that she had made very few of them after *Gone With the Wind*. In 1946 Butterfly bravely turned her back on Hollywood after appearing in *Duel in the Sun*. The actress had grown tired of playing roles she described as "handkerchief heads," and, as early as 1948, her stand against Hollywood stereotyping had been applauded by the British writer Peter Noble in his pioneering book *The Negro in Films*, which I purchased at this time: "For more than a year Butterfly was boycotted by film agents because of her refusal to accept what are described as 'dumb coloured-maid parts,' but she made a brave attempt to establish the right of her people to a just representation in the cinema."[4] What Noble could not have known in 1948 was that Butterfly's sacrifice was in vain, for she never made another Hollywood movie. Her stand against Hollywood echoed an earlier one made by the popular African American singer and actor Paul Robeson. In the *New York Times* (September 24, 1942), after playing a sharecropper in a segment of Twentieth Century Fox's *Tales of Manhattan*, Robeson expressed his dissatisfaction with the film's portrayal of African Americans and vowed he would never make another film in Hollywood: "It turned out to be the same old thing—the Negro solving his problem by singing his way to glory. This is very offensive to my people. It makes the Negro child-like and innocent and is in the old plantation tradition. But Hollywood says you can't make the Negro in any other role because it won't be box office in the South. The South wants its Negroes in the old style."[5] However, unlike Robeson, Butterfly does not appear to have been completely forgiven for playing Prissy. And yet, most major black stars who have played roles that would now be considered "politically incorrect" have been "forgiven." It seems hard to believe that important trailblazing stars like Paul Robeson (in *Sanders of the River*, 1935, and *Tales of Manhattan*) and Sidney Poitier (in *Porgy and Bess*, 1959) were unable to avoid stereotyped roles early in their careers, but they had to start somewhere.

Soon after reading Peter Noble's and Donald Bogle's pioneering books, I discovered another that gave me further insights into the world of Butterfly. In 1972 Edward Mapp published *Blacks in American Films: Today and Yesterday*, a critical study of African American popular cinema. Mapp analyzed numerous films that had been released in America from the silent era, with particular emphasis, year by year, on those released from 1962 to 1970. He dedicated his book to Butterfly:

> Generations of moviegoers remember Prissy, the simple-minded black servant girl who evoked the wrath of Scarlett O'Hara in the baby delivery sequence of *Gone With the Wind*. The author recollects a chance meeting in 1952 with the actress who played Prissy. He recalls as well his subsequent involvement in her project at that time, a new concept of William Shakespeare's *A Midsummer Night's Dream*. Unfortunately this production was never realized. Reading the part of Demetrius under her direction, one soon discovered the full range of her acting ability. It became clear at once that this gifted black actress possessed a mastery of the English speaking language remote from the "who dat say dat?" kind of dialogue assigned her in American motion pictures. The story unfolded in the following pages is part hers and she is in part it. Therefore this book is dedicated to Butterfly McQueen.[6]

At first I had very little knowledge of what happened to her after she left Hollywood, and no way of finding out if she was still alive. Then, at the end of the decade, I had a break. In my local reference library I discovered an entry for her in an edition of *Who's Who in the Theatre*. This gave details of her theatrical career and a contact address in New York: 29 Mount Morris Park West, New York, NY 10027, USA.

I wrote a fan letter to Butterfly McQueen. I did not expect a reply, but to my great surprise—and delight—a postcard arrived from her. It was dated

October 4, 1980. She wrote, "Dear Mr. Bourne, Thank you for nice letter. Hope this finds all well with you. I'm busy as usual. As soon as I write re Hollywood, will remember to send you leaflets. Have only written re Broadway and Harlem. Best always B. McQueen." She gave her address as 405 West 147th Street, New York City 10031.

Meanwhile, my friendships with Robin Mukerji and Ken Sephton, two enthusiastic British moviegoers and collectors of memorabilia from the golden age of Hollywood, proved helpful. Robin and Ken had friends in America who often sent them packages of press clippings about the older generation of movie stars they admired. Any that featured Butterfly were generously passed to me, and I was thrilled to receive them. From these I learned about Butterfly's theatrical pursuits in the 1970s and 1980s (see chapter 9). One that stood out—and was most revealing—was John S. Patterson's review of Butterfly's nightclub act in New York in 1978. He called it "Butterfly McQueen's Lesson in Hanging On":

> She was brought to prominence and sustained there on the strength of one performance, as Prissy, in one film—*Gone With the Wind*, but was unable to sustain a profitable theatrical career after the mass love affair with that schizophrenic civil war fantasy had cooled. With Butterfly McQueen, there are really two shows going on, two performers onstage: the talented, rambling, present day actress Butterfly McQueen, as she perceives herself and Prissy-Hollywood-nostalgia old-time black. Her presence also thrusts before our eyes the painful reminders of the history of blacks and women in film and American life. This is a tall order for a nightclub act. What becomes all too clear as the evening progresses is that Hollywood chewed up a considerable talent as raw material for an image which satisfied the peculiar tastes of 1930's movie producers. Also clear is that the absurd and tenderly comical humanity which shines through that image was a generous gift from Ms. McQueen's rich inner life. That she avoided the destruction which was the lot of others from her early days is indicative of the rare spirit with which she approaches life.[7]

After becoming a professional writer, I felt I had enough material about Butterfly to put into an article for *The Voice*, a national black newspaper that had been launched in 1983. The first article I had published in *The Voice* on January 14, 1984, profiled Butterfly's *Gone With the Wind* costar Hattie McDaniel. Later that year, on September 1, *The Voice* published my tribute to Butterfly. Unlike *Ebony* magazine's negative reaction to Donald Bogle's proposal to celebrate "old timers," the arts editor of *The Voice* supported and encouraged my efforts to write nostalgic stories about the struggles of the older generation of black movie stars. At the same time the paper gave equal coverage to then-newcomers like Whoopi Goldberg and Eddie Murphy.

In the 1970s I started collecting as many books as I could find (and afford) about David O. Selznick and *Gone With the Wind*. Each one I purchased gave me fascinating insights into the complicated history and production of the film, but with only a few exceptions, they barely mention or acknowledge Butterfly. William Pratt's *Scarlett Fever: The Ultimate Pictorial Treasury of "Gone With the Wind"* (1977) is one of the best. Featuring more than five hundred photographs from Herb Bridges's *Gone With the Wind* collection, Pratt includes several previously unpublished shots of Butterfly in costume tests. One of these shows her on the set with Hattie McDaniel. They look happy and relaxed. Other highlights in the book include a useful chronology of the filming, with several mentions of Butterfly. All I can find in Judy Cameron and Paul J. Christman's lavishly produced *The Art of "Gone With the Wind": The Making of a Legend* (1989) is a single, tiny photograph of Butterfly, but it was a rare one, taken on the set in her Prissy costume, with her black dresser. There is no mention of her in the text. Helen Taylor's thoroughly researched and extremely useful *Scarlett's Women: "Gone With the Wind" and Its Female Fans* (1989) includes three pages about Butterfly and Prissy, and the author uses my 1984 article in *The Voice* as one of its sources. Adrian Turner mentions Butterfly several times in *A Celebration of "Gone With the Wind"* (1990) and includes one great colour shot. Butterfly is barely acknowledged in Aljean Harmetz's otherwise sumptuous *On the Road to Tara: The Making of Gone With the Wind* (1996).

Meanwhile, in 1986, I received some unexpected news: Butterfly McQueen was making a movie comeback! It was announced that she had been cast in a supporting role in *The Mosquito Coast*, directed by Peter Weir and starring Harrison Ford and Helen Mirren. I had to wait patiently, until 1987, for the film to be released in Britain, but I was disappointed with her tiny role in Weir's film. If you blinked, you missed her! The following year *Films and Filming* magazine sent me to interview Robert Townsend, a young black film director from America who was in London promoting his new comedy film, *Hollywood Shuffle*. The film exposed the difficulties faced by African American actors trying to break into the film industry, when the only roles on offer seem to be slaves, butlers, pimps, and gang members. During our interview, I spoke to Townsend about the way Butterfly had been wasted in *The Mosquito Coast* and asked him why filmmakers, black and white, overlooked her. He explained that many Americans, especially filmmakers, were still uncomfortable with Butterfly's screen image as Prissy, the "simple-minded darkie," from *Gone With the Wind*. However, Townsend proved to be extremely knowledgeable about black film history and the struggles of black "old timers."

One of Townsend's interests is black American film history, and he is aware of the struggles of the many talented black artists who went out to Hollywood in the 1930s and 1940s and were forced to "shuffle." He says: "Back then the fight was even harder for dignity and for quality roles. But when I see stuff *now*, and they *still* have black people talking that way in 1988, I say nothing has changed. There are still the maids, the butlers and the black buddy sidekick to the white hero. It still happens. Hollywood hasn't changed. The only movie to come out last year with a black cast was *Hollywood Shuffle*." When Townsend, as Bobby Taylor (in *Hollywood Shuffle*), sacrifices his movie career by refusing to play a pimp, his stand is reminiscent of those taken by Paul Robeson and Butterfly McQueen in the 1940s. Says Townsend: "History is lost. A lot of people aren't aware of the stands taken by Mr. Robeson and Miss McQueen. Now, with *Hollywood Shuffle*, people understand what I'm talking about. It's the same thing. People think that Hollywood is very glamorous. I remember the first time I auditioned for a pimp. I thought it was great. Then when I played a pimp for the thirty-ninth time, I thought 'Hey, is this it?' I began to hate my life."[8]

I corresponded with Butterfly throughout the 1980s. In her letters she politely addressed me as "Mr. Bourne." Mostly she sent me notes with flyers about appearances she was making in the United States in her one-woman shows. For example, one flyer, sent in 1981, reads: "*Prissy and Pals* will entertain you in the Harlem State Office Building's Art Gallery on West 125th Street and Adam Clayton Powell Jr. Boulevard (7th Avenue). Songs, Poems, Dance, A Surprise? Questions and Answers. Donations (if able): Adults $2.50 Children 50 cents." I wished I could have traveled to New York, just to see *Prissy and Pals*. She also repeated in her letters her hopes to visit Britain to make a personal appearance, "and I can answer all your and others' questions! Please wait to see if we should even meet in person and have a chat!"[9] Sadly, she never made it to London to make that personal appearance. If she had, Butterfly would have been a sellout and we British fans would have given her a standing ovation!

In 1989, during the fiftieth anniversary celebrations of *Gone With the Wind*, Butterfly did, finally, visit these shores, but regrettably, it was not possible for us to meet. Her visit took her to Edinburgh to make a personal appearance at a screening of *Gone With the Wind* at the Edinburgh Film Festival. I couldn't afford the long and expensive train journey from London to Edinburgh, or the hotel expenses. However, I had recently become acquainted with the festival's director, David Robinson, and he sensed how disappointed I must be feeling. No sooner had Butterfly's visit come to an end than I received a signed photograph from her. It is one of my treasured possessions.

After her death in 1995 (see afterword), I still wanted Butterfly to receive the respect and admiration she deserved, but this has proved impossible without the publication of a biography. I am hoping this modest tribute will help. However, reissues and revivals of *Gone With the Wind* have ensured that generation after generation are introduced to Prissy—and Butterfly. For example, Warner Brothers' recent four-disc DVD release in 2004 has given an opportunity for a new generation to see her and for others to visit an "old friend." These include my friend, the film historian Keith Howes, who, on viewing the film again in 2006, makes the following observations:

My friend Nicholas and I watched the Prissy scenes together on Sunday (Mother's Day in Australia: May 13!). We both agreed that Butterfly Mc-Queen's performance is subtly subversive. The intelligent use of stupidity together with the passive aggression of laziness are, of course, present in the writing and direction but Butterfly McQueen gives them an edge, the absence of which would have made this character a squawking irritation instead of a welcome irritant to the usually self-possessed and controlling Scarlett. We particularly enjoyed the quality of queenly intransigence Butterfly McQueen gives to her line about "only having two hands" upon arrival back at Tara.

We noticed the lack of close-ups given to Prissy as distinct from Mammy: obviously a much more central character in the story but, nevertheless, Prissy is also integral to events leading up to the leaving of Atlanta and to the return home to Tara. Maybe there were close-ups but they were just too overpowering and upstaging for so lowly a personage!

Afterwards I read aloud all Prissy's scenes from the novel to Nicholas. Prissy has a lot more dialogue, all of it in patois and often virtually incomprehensible; however, her scenes and the interactions with Scarlett are quite similar to those in the completed film. What has been added, and it is a delight, is her pleading with Rhett Butler—he leaning out of the brothel window, she in the street below—to come to the rescue. Her squealing and flopping to the ground in a state of supposedly uncontrollable hysteria is the equivalent of Aunt Pittypat's regular attacks of the vapours.

The book also lacks Prissy's sticking out her tongue at Scarlett and a myriad of body, facial and vocal nuances that make Prissy so much more than "a simple-minded darkie."

Seeing Prissy for the umpteenth time was like meeting an old friend. And like some old friends there are things about her I love and things about her that exasperate: essentially, though, I like her spirit, her obstinacy and, above all, her anarchy. In Prissy's case, being a dumb cluck is an art, probably just as studied and perfected as the airs and flirtatious graces of her cruel mistress.

A thought: maybe I and other gay men react so positively to Prissy [because] society sees us as dumb and inconsequential so sometimes we play it that way, especially with straight men who try to eyeball us and put us down. David Rabe's play *Streamers* (filmed 1983) has a Prissy type (white) gay man who causes straights no end of stress. In a way, Quentin Crisp was an unreadable, I'll say anything you want, kind of "servant" who was really the master.[10]

Notes

1. Stephen Bourne and Esther Bruce, *Aunt Esther's Story* (London: Hammersmith and Fulham Ethnic Communities Oral History Project, 1996), 7.

2. Donald Bogle, *Toms, Coons, Mulattoes, Mammies and Bucks: An Interpretive History of Blacks in Americans Films* (New York: Bantam Books, 1974), 125, 127.

3. Bogle, *Toms*, vii.

4. Peter Noble, *The Negro in Films* (London: Skelton Robinson, 1948), 169.

5. Paul Robeson, "Hollywood's Old Plantation Tradition Is Offensive to My People," *The New York Times*, September 24, 1942, quoted in *Paul Robeson Speaks: Writings, Speeches, Interviews 1918–1974*, Philip S. Foner, ed. (London, Melbourne, New York: Quartet Books, 1978), 142.

6. Edward Mapp, *Blacks in American Films: Today and Yesterday* (Metuchen, N.J.: Scarecrow Press, 1972), iv.

7. John S. Patterson, "Butterfly McQueen's Lesson in Hanging On," *The Villager*, August 10, 1978, 7.

8. Stephen Bourne, "Hollywood's Robin Hood," *Films and Filming*, April 1988, 21.

9. Butterfly McQueen, letter to Stephen Bourne, June 27, 1981.

10. Keith Howes, by e-mail, July 4, 2006.

CHAPTER ONE

~

Before Butterfly Became Prissy

> You're too old—too fat—and too dignified for the part. You could never be Prissy.
>
> —Mr. Bundamann (David O. Selznick's representative)

Butterfly was born Thelma MacQueen on January 8, 1911, in Tampa, a United States city in Hillsborough County, on the west coast of Florida.[1] The word *Tampa* is a Native American word that was used to refer to the area when the first European explorers arrived in Florida. Thelma was the only child of Wallace MacQueen, a stevedore on the Tampa docks, and Mary, whose maiden name was Richardson, who worked as a domestic servant.

From the time she could first walk, Thelma loved to dance and sing. She was a natural mimic and at an early age learned the British accent of members of the British-Caribbean community in which she was raised. Her parents sometimes left her with people from Nassau. "That's why you can hear a little touch of British accent in me," she later said.[2] She claimed that she never had any aspirations to be in show business; "however, one day in our backyard in Tampa, I picked up an old magazine of the *Photoplay* type and a strange premonition came over me, letting me know that some day, I, too, would be among those photos I saw in that magazine."[3] She also explained that "amateur theater was always my pastime hobby. I first began as a child in church, reciting books of the Bible every Friday night in chapel. My interest in the theater sprang from the church. All I knew as a child was church, church, church."[4]

Young Thelma's first serious brush with the world of theatre occurred when she took part in a school "playlet" entitled *Aunt Sophronia at College*. Thelma loved dancing, and in the playlet she danced in the "Butterfly Ballet." She later recalled, "We had on beautiful gold tights—and wings with spangles! Oh, it was the loveliest ballet you ever did see."[5] William Shakespeare also entered her life when she danced around the Maypole as the Queen of the Fairies in a school production of his comedy *A Midsummer Night's Dream*. Shakespeare would later figure in some of her adult theatrical endeavors.

There was sadness in Thelma's life when her parents' marriage ended. She was just five years old: "Daddy left us when I was quite young. I can remember him hanging over me at the train station, trying to take me away from Mommy. But the judge said to give me to my Mommy. Later, they hung a tag on me and sent me to Augusta by train, until my Mommy could send for me."[6] In order to support herself and her daughter, Thelma's mother sought full-time employment in a number of cities up and down the East Coast, sending the child to live with an uncle and aunt. The 1920 United States census reveals that Thelma, age eight years and one month, was living in Augusta, Richmond County, Georgia, with her uncle, James Richardson (probably her mother's brother), a waiter in a hotel, and his wife, Ida, a cook for a private family.

In Augusta, Georgia, Thelma's education continued at the Walker Baptist Institute, named after Dr. Charles T. Walker, a former slave who boldly denounced the second-class citizenship of African Americans decades before Dr. Martin Luther King Jr. and Malcolm X were born. He inspired thousands to convert to Christianity and was the founder of one of the most prominent churches in Augusta. Thelma then attended St. Benedict's Convent. After Mary MacQueen took a job as a cook up north in Harlem, New York City, she sent for her daughter to join her. It was here that Butterfly attended Public School 9 on West Eighty-third Street and high school in Babylon, Long Island, New York. The 1930 United States census reveals that Thelma was living and working in Babylon, Suffolk County, Long Island, as a servant to a white family, John E. Wood, a building contractor, his wife, Mary, and their son, John.

After her graduation from high school, Thelma entered the Lincoln Training School for Nursing in the Bronx, but she was distressed by some of the things she observed and flunked her chemistry course. Discouraged, she quit the nursing course and considered other options. A teacher suggested that she try acting, but Thelma worked as a children's nurse and in a factory before taking the plunge. It was an ambitious decision at a time when opportunities for black actors were extremely rare.

First, Thelma joined a dramatic group of the New York Urban League, and it was around this time that she adopted the name Butterfly. It happened like this. In 1934 Thelma joined Miss Venezuela Jones's Negro Youth Theatre Group in Harlem and was cast in a production of *A Midsummer Night's Dream*, staged at New York City College. When the members of the group practiced at the Heckscher Foundation and the Lafayette Theatre, some of them would boast about their professional work in Broadway shows and nightclubs. However, Thelma could only say, "I was in the Butterfly Ballet." Her friend Ruth Moore, who was also a member of group, listened to Thelma as she described her early appearance in the "Butterfly Ballet" of the school playlet *Aunt Sophronia at College*. Ruth then suggested that she take Butterfly as her professional name. Friends immediately began to call her "Butterfly," and she adopted the name as her own. It is not known when Thelma altered the spelling of her surname from MacQueen to McQueen, but it was the latter spelling she used for all her professional theatrical assignments.

So far it has been impossible to verify some of Butterfly's early stage appearances. One source claims that, while working with the Federal Theatre Project, she appeared in *Horse Eats Hat*, a French farce, directed and co-adapted (from *Un chapeau de paille d'Italie*) by Orson Welles. Joseph Cotten and Arlene Francis were in the cast.[7] This opened on Broadway at Maxine Elliott's Theatre on September 26, 1936. *Who's Who in the Theatre* claims that Butterfly made her stage debut in *Brother Rat* at the Biltmore Theatre on December 16, 1936.[8] However, most sources claim that during an audition with the important and influential Broadway producer George Abbott, she impressed him not only with her unusual name but also with her wonderful, high-pitched, childlike voice. Legend has it that Abbott created a role for her as Lucille, an overly genteel parlor maid to a nightclub owner, in his production of Bernie Angus's melodrama *Brown Sugar* (formerly known as *Home Sweet Harlem*), which opened at the Biltmore on December 2, 1937. Says Charles Stumpf, "In one memorable scene she simpered in at the door and announced the arrival of some tough looking thugs. 'Kindly step forward!' she piped up in her tiny voice. . . . It convulsed the audience. One critic noted that her intonation was 'that of a cherub joyfully ushering newcomers through the Pearly Gates.'"[9] *Brown Sugar* lasted only four performances, but in spite of its brief run, it is now remembered for launching Butterfly—with her nervous energy and squeaky voice—into a theatrical career, and the play is often credited as her "official" stage debut. She was, in fact, "the standout in this otherwise lackluster drama of the Harlem underworld."[10]

Brown Sugar was not one of George Abbott's most successful productions, but his next one was, and he made sure Butterfly was in the cast. It was as if she had become Abbott's good luck charm. Clifford Goldsmith's *What a Life*, which opened at the Biltmore on April 13, 1938, was a hilarious comedy about Henry Aldrich, a squeaky-voiced high schooler who is always in trouble. The role of Aldrich was perfectly played by Ezra Stone, and he became such a popular character that he ended up on a successful radio series and, years later, on television. Eddie Bracken and Betty Field were also in the cast of *What a Life*, which ran for 538 performances.

In the middle of this early success, Butterfly was both surprised and delighted to receive an invitation from George Jean Nathan, then president of the New York Drama Critics' Circle, and the leading American drama critic of his time, to be his special guest at a gala dinner at the famous 21 Club. Unfortunately, Butterfly does not mention this in any interviews, but it would be interesting to know if she was the first black woman to be invited to such an event. Nathan was a renowned man about town, and the model for the acerbic Addison De Witt, played by George Sanders in the film *All About Eve* (1950).

Butterfly's next role would not only make her world famous but would change her life forever. Margaret Mitchell's novel *Gone With the Wind* is set in the Old South, and the main characters are a feisty heroine, Scarlett O'Hara, who lives on a plantation called Tara, and a handsome adventurer called Rhett Butler. The Scarlett/Rhett romance is set during the Civil War of 1861–1865 and Reconstruction. The many supporting characters include a young slave called Prissy, who is presented as nothing more than a racial caricature. After hitting the bookstores on June 30, 1936, *Gone With the Wind* immediately became a best seller, and on May 3, 1937, Mitchell received the Pulitzer Prize. For over seventy years, the book has been regarded as a classic; however, criticisms have always been aimed at Mitchell's racial stereotyping.

Prissy is a fictional descendant of Topsy. This controversial racial caricature first appeared in Harriet Beecher Stowe's novel *Uncle Tom's Cabin*, published in 1853, before slavery had been abolished in the United States. It became the best-selling novel of the nineteenth century and the second-best-selling book of the nineteenth century after the Bible. Its antislavery stance is believed to have helped encourage the abolitionist cause in the 1850s. This led to the Civil War of the 1860s that ended slavery in America's Southern states. The story focuses on Uncle Tom, a noble, long-suffering Christian slave. However, Uncle Tom has come to represent African Americans who are accused of "selling out" to whites. "Uncle Tom" has been used as a term of abuse, and in her latter years, Butterfly found herself subjected to this name-calling on the streets of Harlem by other African Americans (see afterword). In spite of its antislavery stance, the book created a number of stereotypes about African Americans that were perpetuated in popular fiction and films for many decades. These stereotypes included the pickaninny image of black children, believed to have originated with the character of Topsy in *Uncle Tom's Cabin*.

Topsy is a young slave girl, aged about eight or nine, of unknown origin. She claims to have "just growed":

> She was one of the blackest of her race; and her round, shining eyes, glittering as glass beads, moved with quick and restless glances over everything in the room. Her mouth, half open with astonishment at the wonders of the new master's parlor, displayed a white and brilliant set of teeth. Her woolly hair was braided in sundry little tails, which stuck out in every direction. The expression of her face was an odd mixture of shrewdness and cunning, over which was oddly drawn, like a kind of veil, an expression of the most doleful gravity and solemnity. She was dressed in a single filthy, ragged garment, made of bagging; and stood with her hands demurely folded before her. Altogether, there was something odd and goblin-like about her appearance—something, as Miss Ophelia afterwards said: "so heathenish," as to inspire that good lady with utter dismay; and, turning to St. Clare, she said: "Augustine, what in the world have you brought that thing here for?"[11]

Topsy was a naughty, unruly little girl who was transformed in the novel by the love of the God-fearing, angelic white child, Little Eva. It is likely that Margaret Mitchell was influenced by her when she created the character of Prissy in *Gone With the Wind*. However, Prissy was most definitely *not* transformed by Scarlett O'Hara, and throughout the novel she remained an objectionable caricature of a young black girl.

Gone With the Wind begins in 1861 at Tara when Scarlett O'Hara is just sixteen years old. In an early scene in the novel, her father, Gerald, has visited John Wilkes's neighbouring Twelve Oaks plantation to purchase Dilcey, a slave who is described as "the head woman and mid-wife" who had recently married Gerald's longtime valet, Pork. Along with Dilcey, Gerald has purchased her twelve-year-old daughter, Prissy, so the two could live on the same plantation. However, Gerald complains that the price (three thousand dollars) has "ruined" him. Scarlett, who is not impressed with Dilcey's daughter, responds, "You didn't need to buy Prissy . . . she's a sly, stupid creature." Scarlett is further unimpressed when Dilcey offers her Prissy as her personal maid.[12]

By purchasing Prissy from John Wilkes, Gerald has avoided mother and daughter being separated. Is this an attempt by Margaret Mitchell to "humanize" him? Is this act of kindness supposed to win sympathy for Gerald after he has taken part in this callous transaction? This can hardly be the case when Mitchell describes Prissy: "She was a brown little creature, with skinny legs like a bird and a myriad of pigtails carefully wrapped with twine sticking stiffly out from her head. She had sharp, knowing eyes that missed nothing and a studiedly stupid look on her face."[13] No wonder Scarlett balked at Dilcey's offer to have Prissy as her maid.

Three years later, during the 1864 siege of Atlanta, Scarlett relies on Prissy's assistance with the imminent arrival of Melanie's baby. Prissy has reminded Scarlett that her mother, Dilcey, was a midwife, and claims that she knows how to deliver babies, too. Speaking in dialect that can only be described as incomprehensible, Prissy reassures her mistress: "Miss Scarlett, effen we kain git de doctah w'en Miss Melly's time come, doan you bodder. Ah kin manage. Ah knows all 'bout birthin'. Ain' mah ma a midwife? Ain' she raised me ter be a midwife, too? Jes' you leave it ter me."[14] Foolishly, Scarlett takes the girl seriously ("Scarlett breathed more easily knowing that experienced hands were near"). Did Mitchell really expect her readers to believe that Scarlett trusted the word of the girl she had earlier described as sly and stupid? This is, after all, the same Prissy who is described in this section of the book as "squalling at the top of her voice" when the Yankees attack Atlanta and who is "reduced to teeth-chattering idiocy" at every unexpected sound.

In the middle of this chaos, there is one poignant moment. While preparing breakfast, Prissy sings "My Old Kentucky Home."[15] This had been written by Stephen Foster in 1853 to describe the thoughts of an elderly slave who has been sold but yearns to be back on his old plantation and with "the old folks at home." The African American abolitionist Frederick Douglass saw the song as sympathetic to slaves. It is the only time in the novel when Prissy expresses something about her terrible condition, but it is unlikely this was Mitchell's intention.

For Scarlett, the situation with Prissy deteriorates when, at the crucial moment when Melanie goes into labor, the terrified girl admits that she knows nothing about midwifery:

> Prissy's mouth fell open and her tongue wagged wordlessly. She looked at Scarlett sideways and scuffed her feet and twisted her thin body. . . . Fright and shame were in her rolling eyes. . . . "Fo' Gawd, Miss Scarlett! We's got ter have a doctah. Ah—Ah—Miss Scarlett, Ah doan know nuthin' 'bout bringin' babies. Maw wouldn' nebber lemme be 'round folkses whut wuz havin' dem."
> All the breath went out of Scarlett's lungs in one gasp of horror before rage swept her. Prissy made a lunge past her, bent on flight, but Scarlett grabbed

her. "You black liar—what do you mean?". . . . "Ah's lyin', Miss Scarlett! Ah
doan know huccome Ah tell sech a lie. Ah jes' see one baby birthed, an' Maw
she lak ter wo' me out fer watchin."[16]

In anger, Scarlett slaps Prissy: "She had never struck a slave in all her life,
but now she slapped the black cheek with all the force in her tired arm."[17]
It is hardly surprising to discover that the British actress Vivien Leigh, who
was cast as Scarlett O'Hara in the film version of *Gone With the Wind*, did
not like the character who made her into an Oscar-winning, international
movie star: "I never liked Scarlett. I knew it was a marvelous part, but I
never cared for her. I couldn't find anything of myself in her, except for one
line. . . . it was the only thing in the character I could take hold of. It's in
the scene after Frank's funeral, when she gets drunk and tells Rhett how glad
she is her mother's dead and can't see her. . . . I liked her then, and perhaps
at the end."[18]

Butterfly's friend, Ruth Moore, had read *Gone With the Wind* and recommended it to Butterfly: "She ran up to me and said that in today's news was
a story about *Gone With the Wind* and David O. Selznick is going to make
it into a movie and you go down to his Park Avenue [New York] office and
tell them you are Prissy."[19] She approached one of Selznick's representatives,
a Mr. Bundamann, and recommended herself for the role. However, in Mr.
Bundamann's opinion, Butterfly was totally unsuitable, and he turned her
down. "You're too old—too fat—and too dignified for the part," he said.
"You could never be Prissy."[20] Consequently Selznick did not hear about her
attempt to secure a role in his picture. Some time later, Butterfly's successes
on the New York stage in George Abbott's *Brown Sugar* and *What a Life* in
1937–1938 brought her name (and talent) to the attention of David O. Selznick. "Agents came to me in Philadelphia during a matinee of George Abbott's *What a Life* and stuck this contract in front of me and said, 'If you want
to come to Hollywood, sign' at the intermission of our matinee. And I just
wanted to see what Hollywood was. And that attracted me because I wanted
to earn money to pay off my debts."[21] By the time Selznick started filming
at the end of 1938, not only had he screen-tested Butterfly, but offered her
a contract. At the time, Butterfly was unaware that the role of Prissy would
conform to Hollywood's stereotype of the black woman. She later admitted
that, back in 1938, she knew little about slavery and black militancy.[22]

In all the books written about *Gone With the Wind*, no other black actress
is mentioned as having been considered by Selznick for the role of Prissy.
Other likely candidates may have been Lillian Yarbo and Theresa Harris,
both of whom had been working in Hollywood for some years. Harris had

made her Hollywood debut in 1930 and had appeared in more than thirty films before she played Zette, Bette Davis's lively but obedient and well-mannered young servant girl, in *Jezebel* (1938; see chapter 6). Harris was about the same age as Butterfly, and she could have been a serious contender, but there is no published record of her being considered, auditioned, or tested. Butterfly herself revealed that the wife of Oscar Polk, who portrayed Gerald O'Hara's manservant Pork in the film, was up for the part, "but she was much too pretty. She was a pretty mulatto girl."[23] It seems that, after Selznick had auditioned and screen-tested Butterfly in New York, he had found Prissy.[24]

Notes

1. An attempt to access a copy of Butterfly McQueen's birth certificate was denied by the records department in Florida because they have a hundred-year rule that has to be enforced before records are released. However, genealogist Deborah Montgomerie has located a copy of Butterfly's United States Social Security application dated July 13, 1937, in which the actress enters her name as Thelma MacQueen and her date and place of birth as January 8, 1911, Tampa, Florida. She also enters her parents' names as Wallace MacQueen and Mary Richardson. Please note that some other sources, including the Internet Movie Database, and Wikipedia, the free Internet encyclopedia, incorrectly give Butterfly's date of birth as January 7.

2. Mal Vincent, "Here's to a Beloved Butterfly Who's Gone with the Wind," *The Virginian-Pilot*, December 31, 1995, 7.

3. Michael Gene Ankerich, "Butterfly McQueen," *Hollywood Studio Magazine*, December 1989, 28.

4. Ankerich, "Butterfly McQueen," 28.

5. Charles Stumpf, "Remembering Butterfly McQueen," *Films of the Golden Age*, Spring 1996, 51.

6. Stumpf, "Remembering," 51.

7. Stumpf, "Remembering," 51.

8. Ian Herbert, ed., *Who's Who in the Theatre*, 16th ed. (London: Pitman, 1977), 898.

9. Stumpf, "Remembering," 51.

10. Mona Z. Smith, *Becoming Something: The Story of Canada Lee* (New York: Faber and Faber, 2004), 61. Also in the cast of *Brown Sugar* were two African American actors who made important contributions to cinema: Canada Lee, who, after appearing in Alfred Hitchcock's *Lifeboat* (1944), gave magnificent performances in Robert Rossen's *Body and Soul* (1947) and Zoltan Korda's *Cry, the Beloved Country* (1952), and Juano Hernandez, who was in Clarence Brown's *Intruder in the Dust* (1949).

11. Harriet Beecher Stowe, *Uncle Tom's Cabin* (1853; Secaucus, N.J.: Longriver Press, 1976), 203.

12. Margaret Mitchell, *Gone With the Wind* (1936; London: Macmillan, 1971), 33.

13. Mitchell, *Gone With the Wind*, 64.

14. Mitchell, *Gone With the Wind*, 321.

15. Mitchell, *Gone With the Wind*, 341.

16. Mitchell, *Gone With the Wind*, 357.

17. Mitchell, *Gone With the Wind*, 358.

18. David Shipman, *The Great Movie Stars: The Golden Years* (London: Hamlyn, 1970), 337.

19. Tinkerbelle, "McQueen for a Day," *Andy Warhol's Interview* 4, no. 11, November 1974, 18.

20. Stumpf, "Remembering," 52.

21. Tinkerbelle, "McQueen for a Day," 18.

22. *Variety*, November 24, 1971, 11.

23. Tinkerbelle, "McQueen for a Day," 18.

24. In *Scarlett* (London: Macmillan, 1991), Alexandra Ripley's sequel to *Gone With the Wind*, Prissy is barely mentioned. In chapter 3, her father, Pork, tells Scarlett that, after working as Rhett Butler's valet, he has retired with a "parting bonus" that will enable Prissy to marry. "Prissy ain't no beauty," he says, "and she's going on twenty-five years old, but with a 'heritance behind her, she can catch herself a husband as easy as a pretty girl what got no money."

CHAPTER TWO

~

Gone With the Wind

Now I am happy I did *Gone With the Wind*. I wasn't when I was 28, but it's part of black history. You have no idea how hard it is for black actors, but things change, things blossom in time.

—Butterfly McQueen

Butterfly's journey from New York to Hollywood—and *Gone With the Wind*—began on Sunday, January 15, 1939, and the film's director, George Cukor, called "Action!" for the first time on Thursday, January 26.[1] It was Cukor who was responsible for filming the memorable sequence in which Mammy (Hattie McDaniel) laces up Scarlett (Vivien Leigh) and chastises her for not eating something before attending the barbecue at Twelve Oaks. Butterfly joined them for the filming. In her first scene in the film, she makes her entrance with a tray of food and the line "Mammy, here's Miss Scarlett's vittles."

According to Sunny Lash, who was secretary and friend to Vivien Leigh, Cukor "had a way of making an actress feel very secure. He was affectionate and kind and gentle and loving. Any woman would love to work with George."[2] In Hollywood, Cukor had a reputation as a "woman's director," and by 1939 he had worked with some of the biggest female names in Tinseltown: Tallulah Bankhead, Kay Francis, Constance Bennett, Katharine Hepburn, Marie Dressler, Jean Harlow, Norma Shearer, Greta Garbo, and Claudette Colbert. On the set of *Gone With the Wind* he was adored and trusted by the film's two leading ladies, Vivien Leigh and Olivia de Havilland, who played

Melanie Hamilton, but Cukor's treatment of Butterfly was awful, especially during the famous "birthin'" sequence. Prissy has lied to "Miss Scarlett" about her midwifery skills and falls apart when Melanie goes into labor. Scarlett is horrified when Prissy cries: "Ah don' know nuthin' 'bout birthin' babies!" (now one of the most famous lines in movie history). With Melanie moaning in the background, an angry Scarlett slaps the terrified slave. Harry Wolf, an assistant cameraman, says that when Vivien Leigh started beating Butterfly McQueen, Cukor told Leigh to make it as real as possible. Wolf says, "In the middle of the shot Butterfly McQueen broke out in tears and she says, 'I can't do it! She's hurting me!' And Cukor got very incensed and he said, 'I'm the director and I'll tell you when to cut the shot.'"[3] In the 1988 documentary *The Making of a Legend: "Gone With the Wind"* (see chapter 10), Butterfly remembered "bargaining" with Cukor and promising to scream loudly if Leigh pretended to hit her face, while the noise of the blow was recorded separately and "dubbed" over the shot.

Another version of the "slapping" incident has been given by Roland Flamini in *Scarlett, Rhett and a Cast of Thousands: The Filming of "Gone With the Wind"* (1975): "Vivien Leigh's slaps left nothing to the imagination—especially the recipient—and Butterfly McQueen broke into tears of pain and indignation. 'I can't do it, she's hurting me, she's hurting me. I'm no stunt man. I'm an actress.' Cukor exploded at the interruption; an actress would have continued, no matter what, he shouted. The scene stopped only when he, the director, said so. But the diminutive black actress walked off the set and refused to return until Vivien Leigh had apologized."[4]

Susan Myrick was employed as one of the film's technical advisors. A reporter for the Southern *Macon Telegraph*, she published a series of reports in her newspaper column on the events occurring on and around the set of *Gone With the Wind*. She describes Cukor's behavior towards Butterfly as "teasing" and found it "amusing." She reports in her column: "Cukor has gone Southern with a vengeance and quotes from the book constantly, threatening to sell Butterfly down the river if she doesn't get the action just right or calling a prop man to get the Simon Legree whip. It is all in good fun, of course, and Prissy enjoys the joke as much as any of us."[5] It would be easy to dismiss this as nothing more than camaraderie on the set, with the director and actress having fun. However, Myrick substitutes Butterfly's name with the name of her character. For Myrick, they are interchangeable. Myrick only saw what she wanted to see, and heard what she wanted to hear. It wasn't until the 1970s that Butterfly began to reveal what *really* happened to her on the set. It was a very different version to the one Susan Myrick told her readers. Meanwhile, in an interview in the *New York Times* in 1968, perhaps unable to talk about the horrible things that happened to her, Butterfly remembers only the positive things, and describes everyone she worked with in *Gone With the Wind* as "wonderful": "Olivia made us laugh and laugh. There she'd be, lying on her bed in labor, screaming 'Scarlett! Scarlett!' and as soon as the scene was over, she'd jump up and start telling us all jokes. And Clark Gable was such a considerate gentleman. Did you know that he was a boy scout leader?"[6]

On February 7, because of the unavailability of certain sets, Cukor was forced to jump ahead in the script. He had been filming the birth of Melanie's baby for several days, but script changes concerning Scarlett's treatment of Prissy held up the production. On Wednesday, February 8, Cukor filmed the birth of Melanie's baby in silhouette, but there was friction between him and Selznick over the script. This came to a climax that weekend, and on Monday, February 13, a press statement was released announcing that Cukor was withdrawing from *Gone With the Wind*. He departed from the project on Wednesday, February 15, and the production was shut down for two weeks. In *The Making of a Legend*, Butterfly remembers the conflict between Cukor and Selznick over her reading of the line "Ma says if you put a knife under the bed it cuts the pain in two" during the birth sequence. Cukor wanted Butterfly to say it in an agitated way, but Selznick wanted it said slowly (as it is in the final version). But it is hard to appreciate how these two intelligent, sophisticated men could have even permitted such a reprehensible line to be kept in the script. It's supposed to be funny, but it isn't. It's callous, and cruel, and just serves to demonstrate Prissy's stupidity.

In 1947 Selznick was quoted by Lloyd Shearer in the *New York Times Magazine*: "We [Cukor and himself] couldn't see eye to eye on anything. I felt that while Cukor was simply unbeatable in directing intimate scenes of the Scarlett O'Hara story, he lacked the big feel, the scope, the breadth of the production."[7] Cukor says in Carlos Clarens's *George Cukor* (1976): "I remained very good friends with Selznick till the end. . . . I must say that Selznick got shaky about everybody: he changed Sidney Howard, he changed the cameraman. He probably got shaky about me. Or maybe Gable didn't think that I knew quite how to handle him, though we were very polite to each other."[8] However, several sources claim that the removal of Cukor from *Gone With the Wind* had everything to do with his homosexuality, which made Clark Gable anxious. Says Richard Barrios in *Screened Out: Playing Gay in Hollywood from Edison to Stonewall* (2003): "His struggles on *Gone With the Wind*, and the reasons for his leaving the production, will forever be in dispute. Some historians go for the more gossipy reasons: that Cukor supposedly knew of Clark Gable's secret rough-trade hustler past . . . which eventually made Gable so uncomfortable that he screamed he wouldn't be directed by a fairy and had him discharged. Others cite Cukor's artistic conflicts with . . . control freak David O. Selznick. As with most history, the real story probably is in a tangled combination of these and other factors."[9]

After leaving *Gone With the Wind*, Cukor went to MGM to direct the film version of Anita Loos's adaptation of Clare Boothe Luce's Broadway comedy *The Women*, starring Norma Shearer, Joan Crawford, and Rosalind Russell. Cukor offered Butterfly a tiny, uncredited role as Lulu, the maid on the cosmetics counter. In one of the film's many hilarious scenes, Crystal Allen (Joan Crawford) asks Lulu to cook a meal for her and her lover at her apartment. After warning Crystal, "I'm noted for the bad way I cook," Lulu reluctantly agrees to help, asking, "Will I find anything in that ice box of yours?" Before Crystal can answer, Pat (Veronica Grey) interrupts: "Cobwebs and a bottle of gin!"

In 1973, Butterfly remembered how Cukor, the man Sunny Lash describes as "kind, gentle and loving," had his revenge on the young actress after he and Selznick had parted company. Cukor's behavior towards Butterfly suggests that his "teasing" of her on the set of *Gone With the Wind* was far removed from the lighthearted interplay Susan Myrick claims she witnessed. Says Butterfly:

> *Gone With the Wind* suspended operations temporarily, and Mr. Cukor asked me to be in *The Women* during this interim. The hurt I felt in having Mr. Cukor scream at me for some mistake I made, I remember vividly and will take with me to my grave. I believe his sole purpose in giving me the small part in *The Women* was to have the opportunity to vent his frustrations on me. In the employ of a David O. Selznick, he could not have done such a thing. I remember the look of co-operation (in his hatred) on the face of Anita Loos when he unleashed his fury upon me. Mr. Selznick soon had us again on the set of *Gone With the Wind*.[10]

Could racism have been behind George Cukor's treatment of Butterfly during the filming of *Gone With the Wind*? It is possible his behavior was caused by the enormous pressure he was under and, especially, the interference of David O. Selznick. However, Cukor never lost his temper with Vivien Leigh or Olivia de Havilland, so why did he pick on a black actress? His behavior towards Butterfly on the set of *The Women* is appalling. Why did he cast her as Lulu in *The Women* if he had had problems with her on the set of *Gone With the Wind*? When Cukor worked with Butterfly on the two films, they were rare occasions when the director worked with an African American actress. On studying the casts of his other films, we find that no black actress ever had a major role in any of his films. Louise Beavers has small roles as maids in *Girls About Town* (1931) and *What Price Hollywood?* (1932); in addition to Butterfly, Theresa Harris, Florence O'Brien, and Hattie Noel have bit parts in *The Women* (1939); and Cicely Tyson has a supporting role as Cat in *The Bluebird* (1976), but she didn't get on with Cukor at all. In fact, his biographer, Patrick McGilligan, says that, on location, "she and Cukor agreed on only one thing—they detested each other."[11]

At least Joan Crawford was fond of Butterfly, even though their scene together was minuscule. Six years later they were memorably reunited in *Mildred Pierce* (see chapter 7): "Joan always loved the film [*The Women*] and had an honest admiration for her own work in it. She thought that Rosalind Russell stole the picture (she never had terribly kind things to say about Shearer), and she recalled how much fun it was to work with Russell, Mary Boland, Butterfly McQueen, and Paulette Goddard. . . . 'Cukor did a great job, I did a great job, Roz was sensational,' she remembered."[12] Butterfly recalled in *Variety* that Crawford was "standoffish when we were together in *The Women*, but much more down to earth when we appeared in *Mildred Pierce*."[13]

Victor Fleming replaced George Cukor as the director of *Gone With the Wind*, and he was responsible for the scene outside Belle Watling's bordello with Prissy and Rhett Butler. Following the birth of Melanie's baby, Scarlett sends Prissy to plead with Rhett to bring a horse and wagon so that they can escape the Yankees as Sherman approaches Atlanta. In this scene, Prissy has her second famous line in the film, when she tells Rhett "de Yankees is comin'" before flopping to the ground in terror and screaming when she hears explosions. Butterfly improvised much of this scene, and she's at her most endearing—and funny—in it, especially when Prissy exaggerates her role in the birth of Melanie's baby, telling Rhett that "Scarlett and me, we brung him, but it was mostly me." Fleming also filmed the cotton-picking sequences at the destitute Tara plantation. However, all the scenes featuring Butterfly, Hattie McDaniel, and Oscar Polk were deleted before the film's release. Scarlett's behavior towards the black servants—in keeping with the book—was considered offensive. Meanwhile, another director, Sam Wood, filmed the sequence—shortly before Ashley's return from the war—where Melanie learns from a soldier that her husband had been taken prisoner. Butterfly would later recall—with pride—how she objected to being seen eating watermelon in this sequence: "I was suffering the whole time. I didn't know that they were going to make the movie so authentic, that I'd have to be just a stupid little slave. I'd do anything they asked, but I wouldn't let Scarlett slap me, and I wouldn't eat watermelon. I was very sensitive about that. Of course, thinking about it now, I probably could have had fun just eating that watermelon and spitting out the pips while everyone went by."[14] Butterfly also tried to change other things about Prissy, without success. In the script, Rhett Butler refers to Prissy as a "simple-minded darkie," a term Butterfly found insulting and unnecessary. Her objections were overruled and the line remained in the script. And while the script called for Prissy to have her hair wrapped in a head scarf in the traditional "slave girl" style, Butterfly insisted on substituting colorful bows. Again, her objections were overruled. She voiced her objections when all the black actors were forced to travel in one car to the set, while the white actors rode in several limousines. She also joined several black players—who had smaller roles—in protesting against restroom segregation.

Butterfly was still involved in the production as late as October 1939 when Selznick, in post-production, decided to reshoot Scarlett's journey back to Tara. He felt it had not captured any of the war's tragedy evident in the book, nor shown how close the fighting had come to Tara. Victor Fleming was called in to direct a short sequence in which Butterfly and Vivien Leigh would drive through a battlefield strewn with dead Confederate and Union soldiers. Thirty-five years later, in an interview in *Andy Warhol's Interview* magazine, Butterfly reflected on her *Gone With the Wind* experiences:

> I was the only unhappy one in that film because I didn't know they were going to be so authentic. And Mr. Selznick understood. He was a very understanding man. He knew it was a stupid part and I was an intelligent person and he thoroughly agreed with me that it wasn't a very pleasant part to play. However, I did my best. My very best. And Mammy said, "You'll never come to Hollywood again. You complain too much." One day Clark Gable said to me, "What's the matter, Prissy?" As if to say, "If they're not nice to you around here, I have some pull." But I was just generally unhappy. I didn't want to be that little slave. I didn't want to play that stupid part. I was just whining and crying. I was a stupid girl. That's what Prissy was. Hahahahahaha. . . . But now I get more for a one-night stand on a college campus, twice as much as I did for a full week then. One never knows what the agent received under the table but I received only $200 a week. And Selznick kept me on the payroll longer than anyone because he appreciated my efforts. My contract was for only six weeks, but I was there for almost a full year, just to speak a wild line like "Miss Scarlett! Miss Scarlett!" Clark Gable was a perfect gentleman. And Vivien Leigh worked so hard.[15]

On Thursday, December 14, 1939, the day before the film's world premiere in Atlanta, Georgia, a *Gone With the Wind* ball took place in the city. The guest list was truly remarkable and included Hollywood celebrities, Southern politicians, and wealthy citizens. Noticeably absent were Hattie McDaniel and Butterfly, who were not welcome in the white side of segregated Atlanta society. However, at the ball, as a member of a choir from his father's church, Ebenezer Baptist, ten-year-old Martin Luther King Jr., the future civil rights leader, *was* present, and he learned how white Atlantans loved their Confederate heritage and the days when plantations and slavery flourished in the surrounding countryside: "He witnessed all the fanfare that attended the world premiere of *Gone With the Wind*, which opened in Atlanta on December 15, 1939. White Atlanta quivered with excitement when Clark Gable, Olivia de Havilland, Vivien Leigh and her husband Laurence Olivier, all came to town for the opening. . . . more than 2,000 white Atlantans crowded into Loew's Grand Theater to see what they fantasized was the world of their ancestors portrayed in living color."[16]

David O. Selznick's intention was to bring Hattie McDaniel and Butterfly to the Atlanta premiere. He hoped they would generate publicity by conducting interviews with black newspapers: "But his advisors warned against it, fearing that McDaniel and McQueen would be forced to endure substandard lodging in Atlanta and that such mistreatment in a segregated Southern city would provide fodder for groups antagonistic to the film. Ultimately it was decided that McDaniel and McQueen ought not to go to Atlanta. The risk of alienating white southerners, it was decided, was too great. Hattie McDaniel's photograph was used in programs distributed in New York and Los Angeles but was removed from the program used in Atlanta."[17]

Hattie was not prevented from attending the Academy Awards ceremony at the Coconut Grove of Los Angeles's Ambassador Hotel on February 29, 1940. She had become the first African American to be nominated for an Oscar, and in her category—Best Supporting Actress—her competition was tough. In addition to her costar Olivia de Havilland, the nominees were Geraldine Fitzgerald (*Wuthering Heights*), Edna Mae Oliver (*Drums Along the Mohawk*), and Maria Ouspenskaya (*Love Affair*). Says her biographer, Jill Watts:

> Hattie McDaniel arrived with her handsome escort for the evening. . . . She looked stunning. Cameras flashed as she made her way to the ballroom, exquisitely dressed in a tasteful, rhinestone-studded aqua blue evening gown, white ermine jacket, and a bountiful corsage of white gardenias. . . . When Fay Bainter, the previous year's Best Supporting Actress, took the podium, Hattie McDaniel must have felt a surge of nerves and excitement. This daughter of ex-slaves, who had struggled with poverty and racial oppression, had finally broken into the highest ranks in Hollywood. . . . When Fay Bainter began, the

room fell silent. "It is with the knowledge that this entire nation will stand and salute the presentation of this plaque," she announced, "that I present the Academy Award for the best performance of an actress in a supporting role during 1939 to Hattie McDaniel."[18]

After seeing the film, Margaret Mitchell expressed her disappointment with Butterfly's portrayal of Prissy: "She felt that she had created a character who should be played as 'shiftless' but not as 'stupid.'"[19] However, Mitchell did not object to Scarlett's appalling treatment of Prissy. Instead she revealed a peculiar desire to play the role of the slave herself, who is racially abused and physically assaulted. On August 13, 1937, she wrote: "I have been especially interested in who would play this little varmint, possibly because this is the only part I myself would like to play. For this reason whoever plays Prissy will be up against a dreadful handicap as far as I am concerned, for I will watch their actions with a jealous eye."[20]

Her disappointment with Butterfly was shared by the Southern columnist Nell Battle Lewis, who, in her column in the *Raleigh News and Observer*, also expressed her dissatisfaction:

> The picture's most conspicuous defect was in Prissy; for Prissy, alas, was little more than the black Butterfly from Harlem. Never once did Butterfly Mc-Queen really get into this part, and I doubt that she ever understood what was expected of her. Even Miss Susan Myrick, who, like the rest of us down here, must be well acquainted with Prissy from encounters in real life, could not impart to the Harlem Butterfly the true conception of the lazy, triflin' Negro girl of Miss Mitchell's story. Though inevitably occasionally comic—for even a fluttery, too-stagey Harlem interpretation could not wholly devitalize the part—Prissy was a flat tire. I'm pretty sure that I could have walked through Oberlin and picked out a better Prissy myself.[21]

Contrary to Nell Battle Lewis's opinions, Butterfly understood the part well, and resisted portraying the character as the "lazy, triflin' Negro girl" created by Mitchell. However, faced with her first movie role, in one of the most ambitious productions ever made, the young actress must have been overwhelmed and intimidated by the likes of Cukor and Selznick, and what was going on around her. The fact that she put her own stamp on the character and defiantly stood up to Cukor and Sam Wood (when she refused to eat watermelon in one of the scenes Wood directed) is a testament to her strength of character. In Butterfly's hands, Prissy is much more appealing and waiflike than Mitchell's lazy, stupid character. Against the odds, Butterfly succeeds in creating someone whom Donald Bogle describes as "delicately shaded, puzzlingly ambivalent, madcap, bizarre and off on cloud nine."[22] So, in a way, for upsetting the likes of Southerners like Margaret Mitchell and Nell Battle Lewis with her interpretation of the role of Prissy, Butterfly had the last laugh. Thomas Cripps, in *Slow Fade to Black* (1977), who describes the black actors who worked on *Gone With the Wind* as "professionals and craftsmen," makes the following comments about Butterfly:

> After she gave her cry of "de Yankees is comin'" she plumped down with an anthology of Alexander Woollcott. Always, she balked at treatment less than professional. Cukor expected no more than a quick reading, and when she covered her face and fought to capture a mood, he barked, "Whoja think you are, Greta Garbo?" When the crew aped her trills she smiled them aside and called them "my imitators." And in the end she won in a small way. *Time* noticed her "sly humour," especially when the Yankees come to Atlanta and she sings "Jes' a few mo' days ter tote de wee-ry load."[23]

Notes

1. This chapter could not have been written without the information made available in William Pratt's *Scarlett Fever: The Ultimate Pictorial Treasury of "Gone With the Wind"* (London: Collier MacMillan, 1977).

2. Sunny Lash, interviewed in the television documentary *The Making of a Legend: "Gone With the Wind"* (October 5, 1988).

3. Harry Wolf, in *The Making of a Legend*.

4. Roland Flamini, *Scarlett, Rhett and a Cast of Thousands: The Filming of "Gone With the Wind"* (New York: Andre Deutsch, 1975), 216.

5. Susan Myrick quoted in *White Columns in Hollywood: Reports from the "Gone With the Wind" Sets*, Richard Harwell, ed. (Macon, Ga.: Mercer University Press, 1982), 83.

6. Guy Flatley, "Butterfly's Back in Town," *The New York Times*, July 21, 1968, 18.

7. David O. Selznick quoted in *Memo From: David O. Selznick*, Rudy Behlmer, ed. (New York: Viking Press, 1972), 236.

8. Carlos Clarens, *George Cukor* (London: Secker and Warburg, 1976), 188–89.

9. Richard Barrios, *Screened Out: Playing Gay in Hollywood from Edison to Stonewall* (New York: Routledge, 2003), 161. Other sources that explore the "gossipy reason" for Cukor's "sacking" include Boze Hadleigh, *Conversations with My Elders* (London: Gay Men's Press, 1986); Patrick McGilligan, *George Cukor: A Double Life* (London and Boston: Faber and Faber, 1991); and Raymond Murray, *Images in the Dark: An Encyclopedia of Gay and Lesbian Film and Video* (New York: Plume / Penguin, 1996).

10. Murray Summers, "Butterfly McQueen Was One of The Women Too," *Filmograph* 3, no. 4 (1973), 7–8.

11. Patrick McGilligan, *George Cukor: A Double Life* (London and Boston: Faber and Faber, 1991), 316.

12. Lawrence J. Quirk and William Schoell, *Joan Crawford: The Essential Biography* (Lexington: University Press of Kentucky, 2002), 102.

13. "Butterfly McQueen: Who Knew Her Mind Before 'Stereotype' Discovered," *Variety*, November 24, 1971.

14. Pam Fessler, "Butterfly's Flights of Fancy," *The Record*, April 2, 1978, 21.

15. Tinkerbelle, "McQueen for a Day," *Andy Warhol's Interview* 4, no. 11, November 1974, 18–19.

16. Stephen B. Oates, *Let the Trumpet Sound: A Life of Martin Luther King, Jr.* (New York: Harper and Row, 1982), 11.

17. Gary M. Pomerantz, *Where Peachtree Meets Sweet Auburn: A Saga of Race and Family* (New York: Penguin, 1997), 113.

18. Jill Watts, *Hattie McDaniel: Black Ambition, White Hollywood* (New York: Amistad, 2005), 177–79.

19. Nell Battle Lewis, "Scarlett Materializes," *The Raleigh News and Observer*, February 18, 1940, quoted in Richard Harwell, ed., *"Gone With the Wind" as Book and Film* (Columbia, S.C.: University of South Carolina Press, 1983), 170.

20. Lewis, "Scarlett Materializes," quoted in Harwell, *"Gone With the Wind" as Book and Film*, 170.

21. Lewis, "Scarlett Materializes," quoted in Harwell, *"Gone With the Wind" as Book and Film*, 172.

22. Donald Bogle, "Black Humor: Full Circle from Slave Quarters to Richard Pryor," *Ebony*, August 1975, 33.

23. Thomas Cripps, *Slow Fade to Black: The Negro in American Film, 1900–1942* (London, Oxford, and New York: Oxford University Press, 1977), 361.

CHAPTER THREE

~

Black Resistance to
Gone With the Wind

Hollywood was more segregated than Georgia under the skin. A Negro couldn't do anything straight, only comedy.

—Stepin Fetchit, in Joseph McBride,
"Stepin Fetchit Talks Back," *Film Quarterly*

I'd always loved the movies, even as a little girl, but the way that films like *Gone With the Wind* presented black people drove me crazy. I felt from an early age it was my duty to give black people back their dignity on screen.

—Euzhan Palcy, in Stephen Bourne,
"Far Away from Hollywood," *Black Filmmaker*[1]

African American moviegoers probably found Butterfly McQueen and Stepin' Fetchit less humorous and less compelling than did their white counterparts (although it would be a lie to say that these characters never elicited laughter from the balcony). What historians might explore, in this particular instance, is whether black audiences saw these characters as tricksters; their own words, actions, and gestures reinterpreted as subversive acts in which white folks become the target of ridicule.

—Robin D. G. Kelley, "Notes on Deconstructing
'The Folk,'" *American Historical Review*

For me, it was not enough to dismiss Hattie McDaniel and Butterfly McQueen as mere mammy and pickaninny. Anyone who had seen them in

Gone With the Wind and left the theater with no more than that impression really missed or ignored the strength of the performances, and at the same time denied black America a certain cultural heritage.

—Donald Bogle, *Toms, Coons, Mulattoes,*
Mammies and Bucks: An Interpretive History of Blacks in American Films

In 1984 the film director Steven Spielberg described *Gone With the Wind* as "one of the greatest American movies ever made."[2] The film has also been criticized for being a reactionary glorification of America's Old South and slavery. The film's depiction of African Americans has been commented on before and since its release in 1939. David O. Selznick listened to the concerns of various critics before he started filming. He was persuaded to delete the word "nigger" from the script, and eliminate references to the Ku Klux Klan on the grounds that the inclusion of the Klan "might come out as an unintentional advertisement for intolerant societies in these fascist-ridden times."[3] He also said: "I have gone to extremes in the preparation in casting of the picture to avoid any derogatory representation of the Negroes as a race or as individuals and to eliminate the major things in the story which were apparently found offensive by Negroes in the Margaret Mitchell book. I feel so keenly about what is happening to the Jews of the world that I cannot help but sympathize with the Negroes in their fears about material which they regard as insulting and damaging."[4] And yet, in spite of Selznick's intentions, Leonard Pitts Jr., the nationally syndicated columnist who received the 2004 Pulitzer Prize for Commentary, described the film as "a romance set in Auschwitz."[5] Says Roland Flamini, "If it is too harsh a judgment to say that by their indifference, producers like Selznick actually inhibited the cause of race relations in America, they cannot be said to have acted as the spur and model for greater racial understanding. This is perhaps one of the great missed opportunities of the movies, but at the time Hollywood believed that messages were best left to Western Union."[6]

Further investigation reveals that Selznick took some persuading to delete the word "nigger" from Sidney Howard's script. Margaret Mitchell thought the word harmless, but that isn't surprising. Howard considered Mitchell's black characters as "the best written darkies . . . in all literature."[7] However, Joseph I. Breen, the administrator of Hollywood's Production Code (also known as the Hays Code), who was looking out for his own skin, reminded Selznick that when Lionel Barrymore uttered the word "nigger" in *Carolina* (1934), African American audiences in Chicago, Washington, Baltimore, New York, and Los Angeles had thrown bricks at the screen. At first, Selznick persuaded Breen to permit the black characters, but not the white ones, to use the word "nigger." The black cast members, including Hattie McDaniel and Butterfly McQueen, were upset. The word "nigger" hurt and offended them. Breen overruled Selznick and banned the word "nigger" for *all* characters. Reluctantly, Selznick and Howard changed "nigger" to "darkie" so Rhett refers to Prissy as a "simple-minded darkie." Some progress, eh? When Breen first challenged him about this, Selznick had good reason to be worried. He hadn't forgotten when filming began that some black actors who had been cast in minor roles threatened to leave the production unless the lavatories were desegregated: "They protested that some of the lavatories on the back lot bore freshly painted notices saying WHITES, while others said COLOREDS. They threatened to walk off the production unless the signs were removed."[8] They were removed.

The film's depiction of slavery is simplistic, romanticized, and misleading. With the exception of Prissy, the black servants of the O'Hara family are well-treated, cheerful "darkies," loyal to their benevolent owners, even after slavery has been abolished and they have been given their freedom. It could be argued that the portrayal of the slaves is an improvement on those depicted in D. W. Griffith's controversial silent film epic *The Birth of a Nation* (1915). In Griffith's film they were caricatured—and debased—by white actors in blackface. Selznick's vision of slavery in the Old South doesn't improve that much on Griffith's, for he failed to acknowledge the complex racial issues of the Reconstruction era immediately following the Civil War.

Unlike Scarlett's feisty, outspoken Mammy, *Gone With the Wind* depicts African American men as stupid, emasculated children, such as Gerald O'Hara's servant Pork (Oscar Polk), the field hand Big Sam (Everett Brown), and Uncle Peter (Eddie "Rochester" Anderson). Then there is Prissy, who remains the most controversial black character in the film. When the prominent black nationalist leader Malcolm X wrote his autobiography, he recalled the embarrassment he felt when he saw *Gone With the Wind* as a teenager around 1940: "When it played in Mason, I was the only Negro in the theater, and when Butterfly McQueen went into her act, I felt like crawling under the rug."[9] When he made this comment in the mid-1960s, Malcolm X must have expressed what many African Americans felt about Prissy. Some years later, Alice Walker, the celebrated African American author and feminist, who received the 1983 Pulitzer Prize for Fiction for *The Color Purple*, made public her childhood unhappiness with Scarlett O'Hara, Prissy, and *Gone With the Wind*:

Dear Lucy
    You ask why I snubbed you at the Women for Elected Officials Ball. I don't blame you for feeling surprised and hurt. After all, we planned the ball

together, expecting to raise our usual pisspot full of money for a good cause. Such a fine idea, our ball: Come as the feminist you most admire! But I did not know you most admired Scarlett O'Hara and so I was, for a moment, taken aback. I don't know; maybe I should see that picture again. Sometimes when I see movies that hurt me as a child, the pain is minor; I can laugh at the things that make me sad. My trouble with Scarlett was always the forced buffoonery of Prissy, whose strained, slavish voice, as Miz Scarlett pushed her so masterfully up the stairs, I could never get out of my head.[10]

Malcolm X and Alice Walker made their feelings known in the 1960s and the 1980s, but what is not generally known is that when the film was in production and released in December 1939, its treatment of African Americans was a cause célèbre. *Gone With the Wind* may have provided underemployed black actors and extras with a living and exposure in a major Hollywood production, but shortly after filming commenced, some African Americans who objected to the novel—and its screen adaptation—made their feelings known. For example, in February 1939, the black publisher Leon Washington circulated a petition among African American maids to boycott the film when it was released.[11] The film's premiere in Atlanta coincided with an attack on Hollywood by the *Daily Worker*, a newspaper published in New York City by the Communist Party USA. Says Nancy D. Warfield:

> Ben Davis Jr., a black member of the editorial board, wrote a review claiming that Selznick made the film purely as a propaganda piece which, while defaming the black, also subtly ennobled the moneyed class of the country at the expense of poor whites, factory workers, and blacks (December 24, 1939). In short, GWTW was nothing more than a monstrous glorification of the capitalist system. . . . The truth is that the pro-Southern tone of the novel had been toned down. . . . *The Daily Worker*'s case was, however, very real in this sense; in making the film at all, Selznick opened up a Pandora's box of mischief. . . . Coming as it did on the eve of World War II, *Gone With the Wind* was unavoidably compared to *The Birth of a Nation*, which had been released just prior to our entry into World War I. *The Birth of a Nation* was dredged up by the Communist Party because it hoped to parallel Selznick's treatment of the black with Griffith's. Moreover, Griffith had been subject in 1939 to a particularly vehement attack by pro-communist writers.[12]

Some African Americans felt so strongly about the film that they picketed cinemas that were screening it. One banner said, "You'd Be Sweet Too Under a Whip." On March 9, 1940, the *Afro-American* journal carried four photographs of picketers at the Washington, D.C., premiere, but offset them with two black columnists who supported the film, including Lillian Johnson, who claimed the pickets were either uninformed about the film's content or were trying to mislead customers. She said the film was a "true representation of the period," even if members of her race did not like that representation.[13] In "An Open Letter to Mr. Selznick," dated January 9, 1940, the black dramatist Carlton Moss argues that the film's "falsification of a progressive era in American life" promoted two major lies: "(1) That the Negro didn't care about or want his freedom (2) That he had neither the qualities nor the 'innate' ability to take care of, let alone govern, himself."[14] Says Helen Taylor: "Moss was also appalled by all the Negro characters, describing the line-up as 'shiftless and dull-witted Pork, Young Prissy, indolent and thoroughly irresponsible, "Big" Sam with his radiant acceptance of slavery and Mammy with her constant haranguing and doting on every wish of Scarlett.'"[15]

In his books and articles, Donald Bogle has done more to draw attention to the flip side of African American film actors than anyone. A gifted black film scholar, Bogle has championed Hattie McDaniel and Butterfly McQueen since the early 1970s, while recognizing the limitations imposed on them. Regarding Hattie, he says:

> I was a movie kid. In that snow-white landscape, every now and then I'd see this face of color coming out at me, and I'd be transfixed. The performers had another kind of rhythm and they spoke to us through that rhythm. Take Hattie McDaniel in *Gone With the Wind*. She's a strong figure, powerfully built, with a rich sonic boom of a voice. When you hear her speak, you know she was born to give orders, not to take them. When she talks to Scarlett, she looks her right in the eye. There's nothing really servile about any of her dealings with the white characters. . . . There was another life and point of view that was being suggested to me by Hattie McDaniel's rather hostile edge. . . . Despite the fact that she played servants to white characters, there is a strong sense of self that comes through in her performances. Here is a woman who can't be reduced. Other actresses might not have been able to express this confidence and assuredness. Or do it in the sly way that McDaniel did it, with that half-smile on her face.[16]

A different point of view has been expressed by an unidentified black lesbian whose interview with Claire Whitaker was reprinted in *Jump Cut: Hollywood, Politics and Counter-Cinema*, a collection of articles selected from the film magazine *Jump Cut*. This dynamic journal offered a subversive counterpoint to Hollywood and included articles about radical Third World filmmakers, gays and lesbians, and the independent left. Whitaker's interviewee, referred to as "Gladys," says:

> In terms of being black, there weren't, and still aren't, many roles to identify with. You could be Hattie McDaniel in the role of Mammy, Butterfly

McQueen in the role of stupid, Eartha Kitt in the role of slut, Lena Horne in the role of light-skinned dark woman leaning against a piano and singing songs. Those are the only images you had or really have! Another one is the strong mother like Jane Pittman. I'm not that, I'm not a slut, and I'm not a rag-on-the-head mammy. Whom can I identify with in terms of a black woman in film? . . . The whole film [*Gone With the Wind*] in its portrayal of black women and men is so blatantly racist. They must have spent hundreds of dollars on glycerine to make *all* the black people look greasy. Every black person looked like they had been in 100-degree sun for hours. Everyone cried on Hattie McDaniel's shoulder—that's bull. Almost all Hollywood films are racist, both when they don't have blacks in them and when they do. And they're sexist. It comes from the minds of the people who make them. It's bad news that we have to pay money to go see this schlock. But I do keep going. We have no alternative. And sometimes horrible movies can be really enjoyable because they hit on a certain level.[17]

The African American film director Melvin Van Peebles is famous for his controversial independent feature *Sweet Sweetback's Baadasssss Song* (1971) and for inspiring such radical and innovative black filmmakers as Spike Lee. In 1998, in the documentary *Classified* X, Van Peebles took a witty, ironic, and critical look at the racial stereotyping of African Americans in cinema. Born in Chicago, he recalled going to the local movie house as a youngster and being disturbed by the images he felt were "messing with my mind": "The colored folks in the movies were always quaking and yassuh bossing and shufflin'. They didn't bear any resemblance to the majestic, hard-working black folks struttin' around the south side of Chicago where I was from. The men were tough and fearless and the women were regal queens." Van Peebles added that there was one exception: "The only real hope was Sam. You remember the colored piano player in *Casablanca* [1943]? It was the first time I ever remember seeing a black character go through an entire movie without having to kiss ass. In the ghetto the people were so proud that they would make the projectionist stop the film and run Sam's part over and over and over again." Van Peebles also comments on the treatment of black women in American movies. After he says, "If things were tough for a white woman, they were draconian for a black woman," the documentary cuts to Prissy being slapped by Scarlett O'Hara.[18]

It is doubtful if African American commentators like "Gladys" and Melvin Van Peebles would be convinced by the various appraisals Donald Bogle has offered about Butterfly McQueen and Prissy through the years, and yet Bogle has revealed an insight into black characters in Hollywood movies that is exceptional. It began in 1974 with his first book, *Toms, Coons, Mulattoes,*

Mammies and Bucks: An Interpretive History of Blacks in American Films, in which he gives the following reassessment of Butterfly and *Gone With the Wind*. One can only hope that she read it and realized that her efforts were not in vain and were appreciated:

> Some observers saw Butterfly as the stock darky figure. But there was much more to her performance. Had she been a mere pickaninny, she might have engendered hostility or embarrassed audiences. Instead she seemed to provide an outlet for the repressed fears of the audience. That perhaps explains why everyone laughed hysterically at her hysterics. For during the crisis sequences, the film built beautifully, and there was a need for release. Mere comic relief of the old type would have been vulgar. But because of her artistic mayhem, her controlled fright, and her heightened awareness and articulation of the emotions of the audiences, Butterfly McQueen seemed to flow wonderfully with the rest of the film. She had a pleasant waiflike quality, too, not in the patronizing style of *The Green Pastures*, in which the grown-up people behaved like rambunctious idiot children, but in a special, purely personal way. Tiny and delicate, Butterfly McQueen seemed to ask for protection and was a unique combination of the comic and the pathetic.[19]

One film that Melvin Van Peebles did not mention in *Classified X* was Steven Spielberg's version of Alice Walker's novel *The Color Purple* (1985). Spielberg's description of *Gone With the Wind* ("one of the greatest American movies ever made") was made during the production of his film. Alice Walker had reservations about Spielberg directing *The Color Purple*, but in the end she trusted him and hoped for the best. Regrettably, the film is flawed, and it has not stood the test of time. Its portrayal of African American women is as problematic as *Gone With the Wind*, and the film has generated debates as heated and lively as those around David O. Selznick's epic drama. Whoopi Goldberg, in her first film, gives a brilliant central performance as Celie, but it is hard to understand why Alice Walker could not prevent a work of genius (her novel)—for which she received the Pulitzer Prize—being turned into an overblown, sentimental, and flawed soap opera. Before he made *The Color Purple*, Spielberg had directed some terrific movies for mass audiences, including *Jaws, Close Encounters of the Third Kind, Raiders of the Lost Ark*, and *E.T.*, but he shouldn't have taken on *The Color Purple*. Sheila Johnston, in the London listings magazine *Time Out*, summarized: "Walker's clear, lyrical patois has been filmed with, well, purple pomposity, a battering ram of flashy editing and tearful emotion. Nor is it altogether surprising that he treads delicately round the story's more radical elements, like Celie's lesbian love for free-spirited blues singer Shug (Avery) or the political insights of her sister's African experience. And yet . . . due in no small measure to a superb cast this is a powerful and honourable attempt to wrest an unusual book into the populist, Hollywood mainstream."[20] Dorothy Francis's black female perspective in *Trouble and Strife* (Spring 1987), a "radical feminist magazine," was also perceptive, and makes one realize why *The Color Purple* was not the breakthrough film for African American women that it should—and could—have been. The film's shortcomings make one wonder if Hollywood had moved that far in its portrayal of African American women since 1939 and *Gone With the Wind*. Dorothy Francis says:

> There is a trend in America at present towards the popular mass marketing of Black culture aimed at the ever-hungry white majority. . . . Spielberg is to be found guilty of jumping onto this particular band-wagon as well as cashing in on the current popularity of women's writings. . . . I had the overwhelming impression that after *E.T.* and *Gremlins*, he cast about and thought to himself "What sweet little aliens can I portray next?" . . . The film is far removed from the everyday realities of Black people, it glamourises and glosses over the situation of most American Blacks. . . . Many of the audience, including myself, left with tears in their eyes, but mine were of anger and sadness. I wept with disappointment for what could have been a brilliant and important film.[21]

Notes

1. In 1983 the Martinique-born Euzhan Palcy became the first black woman to direct a feature film, *Rue Cases Negres* (Black Shack Alley). It was an international success and won several awards at the Venice Film Festival, including Best First Film (Silver Lion). It also won the French César for Best First Film.

2. Lewis Beale, "'Gone With the Wind' Can't Shed Its Racism," *Daily News*, March 6, 1989, 21.

3. Roland Flamini, *Scarlett, Rhett and a Cast of Thousands: The Filming of "Gone With the Wind"* (New York: Andre Deutsch, 1975), 184.

4. David O. Selznick, quoted in the American television documentary *The Making of a Legend: "Gone With the Wind"* (October 5, 1988).

5. Wikipedia online biography of Leonard Pitts Jr.

6. Flamini, *Scarlett*, 185.

7. Leonard J. Leff and Jerold L. Simmons, *The Dame in the Kimono: Hollywood, Censorship, and the Production Code from the 1920s to the 1960s* (London: Weidenfeld and Nicholson, 1990), 95.

8. Flamini, *Scarlett*, 216.

9. Malcolm X, *The Autobiography of Malcolm X* (London: Hutchinson, 1966), 113.

10. Alice Walker, "A Letter of the Times, or Should This Sado-Masochism Be Saved?" in *You Can't Keep a Good Woman Down* (London: Women's Press, 1982), 118.

11. Leff and Simmons, *Dame in the Kimono*, 95.

12. Nancy D. Warfield, "GWTW—1939," *The Little Film Gazette of N. D. W* 3, no. 1 (November 1978), 33.

13. John D. Stevens, "The Black Reaction to *Gone With the Wind*," *Journal of Popular Film* 2 (Fall 1973), 370.

14. Carlton Moss quoted in Helen Taylor, *Scarlett's Women: "Gone With the Wind" and Its Female Fans* (London: Virago Press, 1989), 187.

15. Taylor, *Scarlett's Women*, 187.

16. Donald Bogle, "The Defiant Ones," interview with Lisa Jones, *Village Voice Film Special*, June 4, 1991, 69.

17. Claire Whitaker, "Part One: Hollywood: The Dominant Cinema 5. Hollywood Transformed: Interviews with Lesbian Viewers," in *Jump Cut: Hollywood, Politics and Counter-Cinema*, ed. Peter Severn (New York: Praeger, 1985), 116–17.

18. Melvin Van Peebles, *Classified X* (1998), directed by Mark Daniels.

19. Bogle, *Toms*, 126–27.

20. Sheila Johnston, *Time Out* 829, July 9–15, 1986, 32.

21. Dorothy Francis, "A Whiter Shade of Purple," *Trouble and Strife*, Spring 1987, 18–19.

∽

CHAPTER FOUR

Hattie McDaniel:
More Than a Mammy

I'd rather play a maid and make $700 a week, than be a maid for $7.

—Hattie McDaniel

For playing Scarlett O'Hara's faithful mammy in *Gone With the Wind*, Hattie McDaniel became the first black actress to win an Oscar—and the last for over fifty years until Whoopi Goldberg won for her role as the eccentric medium Oda Mae Brown in the romantic comedy *Ghost* (1990). Hattie has become closely identified with the role of the mammy—a passive, one-dimensional, comical, nonthreatening caricature of black womanhood. Yet in the seventy-odd films that made up her career, she also managed to extend, subvert, and confound the Hollywood stereotypes of black women.

The mammy caricature found its first representation in the popular fiction, poetry, and music of the nineteenth century. Aunt Chloe, the mammy in Harriet Beecher Stowe's novel *Uncle Tom's Cabin* (1852), who is described as having "a round, black, shining face. . . . Her whole plump countenance beams with satisfaction and contentment from under her well-starched checked turban," is as good an example as any.[1] Mammy first appeared in Hollywood films in the silent era, including nine versions of *Uncle Tom's Cabin* between 1903 and 1927. Bossy and cantankerous she may be, but her loyalty is never in question, as in D. W. Griffith's Civil War melodrama *The Birth of a Nation* (1915), where the mammy, played by a white actress in blackface, continues as a faithful servant to her former white master even after the Civil War and emancipation.

In the silent era most black roles were played by whites in blackface, but with the coming of sound in the late 1920s, this began to change, and Gertrude Howard was one of the first black actresses to secure roles. For example, she played Aunt Chloe in the 1927 screen version of *Uncle Tom's Cabin* and subsequently found herself typecast as a mammy in a succession of films, including the first film version of *Show Boat* (1929), in which she played Queenie, and *Hearts in Dixie* (1929). Her most famous role was as Mae West's maid and confidante Beulah Thorndike (Gertrude was honored with a surname, too!) in *I'm No Angel* (1933), where she is tossed one of the most famous racist remarks ever made to a black woman in the movies: "Beulah, peel me a grape." Sadly there is nothing in Howard's portrayal of the submissive, scatterbrained Beulah to counteract the racism of the film. However, Howard is given prominence because Mae West insisted on having at least one black maid in every one of her films. Others included Louise Beavers (*She Done Him Wrong*, 1933) and Libby Taylor (*Belle of the Nineties*, 1934). When the director Henry Hathaway asked her the reason, Mae replied: "Lissen, don't forget that one out of every four people in the gallery is colored. They're my public and I gotta show 'em I'm democratic."[2]

Following Gertrude Howard's death in 1934, Hattie McDaniel and Louise Beavers inherited—and shared—her crown as Hollywood's favorite mammy. But unlike Howard, they often defied convention and resisted the stereotype. Louise Beavers had a much longer career in the movies than Hattie. From the late 1920s to the early 1960s, Louise appeared in over 150 films as maids, housekeepers, cooks, and mammies. Says Danny Peary: "Her characters weren't funny, outspoken, bossy, or suspicious of male strangers as were Hattie McDaniel's. . . . They were cheerful, protective, and so loyal that they'd keep working even if their mistresses no longer had the money to pay their salaries."[3]

From her film debut in 1932, Hattie McDaniel stood out because she often managed to breathe life into the mammy stereotype, and the characters she portrayed were rarely completely submissive or subservient. In film after film, especially in the screwball comedies of the 1930s, she gave Aunt Dilsey, Beulah, and Delilah a wide range of moods. Admittedly, she was always cast as a helpful maid and confidante, a loyal, trusted friend to her white mistresses, but where possible she infused her roles with integrity and depth. Through a remarkable effort of interpretation, and with occasional support from directors such as George Stevens and James Whale, her mammies and maids appeared opinionated, defiant, hostile, flamboyant, camp, assertive, and tough.

In her films of the 1930s and 1940s, Hattie matched just about every major Hollywood movie star. In 1932 in *Blonde Venus*, she hides Marlene

Dietrich from a private detective—the first of many roles as friend and protector to a white movie heroine. Black women as confidantes (but not social equals) were featured in numerous Hollywood films of the time, the typical example being Louise Beavers as "Aunt" Delilah Johnson in *Imitation of Life* (1934). But Hattie's movie servants were different. In *Alice Adams* (1935), Katharine Hepburn plays a small-town social climber who wants to impress the son of a wealthy family. She invites him to dinner and hires gum-chewing Malena Burns (Hattie) to cook and serve the meal. Director George Stevens makes clever use of Hattie to comment on, and make fun of, Hepburn and her family—as Donald Bogle describes it: "Thus was fixed, in this film, the nature of Hattie McDaniel's relations with her white masters. Through her uproarious conduct, she puts them in their place without overtly offending them. . . . she struts about looking down on them, all the while pretending to be the model servant. . . . thirties audiences knew Hattie McDaniel was putting them on."[4] There is further evidence of this in the way Hattie delivers her two lines of speech. Unlike most black characters in 1930s Hollywood movies, she says "the" instead of "de."

In most of these films Hattie behaves familiarly with white players, a rare occurrence for a black actor in Hollywood movies at the time. For example, in *China Seas* (1935), when her employer Jean Harlow asks her if she looks like a lady, Hattie replies: "I've bin with you too long to insult you that way!" In *Saratoga* (1937), Hattie reveals her sexual attraction to Harlow's leading man (Clark Gable). "I'd fix up for him anytime," she says. "If only he was the right color, I'd marry him!" In *The Mad Miss Manton* (1938), she roughly dismisses a (white) telegram boy from Barbara Stanwyck's apartment with the words: "OK, child. You'd think they'd send an older man up to this apartment"—an assertive wit no real-life black maid would have risked. And there is nothing subtle about her delivery when she answers white people back, as in *Show Boat* (1936), where she turns on a docker who tells her to get out of his way with the retort: "Who wants to get in your way?" In *The Shopworn Angel* (1938), as maid to Margaret Sullavan, she is incorporated into the narrative, functioning in the drama as well as in the comedy, a status attributed to no other contemporary black movie servant.

As Queenie in *Show Boat*, for the director James Whale, an Englishman who was also a "socially displaced" Hollywood figure because of his homosexuality, Hattie shows many facets of her talent. Physically and temperamentally she is the opposite of her husband Joe (Paul Robeson): while she is small, rotund, quick-tempered, tough, and aggressive, he's a passive, towering presence, a tall, gentle giant. The two performances complement each other beautifully, with Robeson appearing relaxed and charming when he is supposed to look stupid and shuffling. Hattie's campness comes through not only in her performance and posture (especially in the song "Can't Help Lovin' That Man"), but in her appearance: the jewelry (brooch, rings, large dangling earrings), the gigantic, ludicrous bandanna, the carefully manicured fingernails. All this appears to be a deliberate attempt on the part of Hattie and her director James Whale to send up the stereotype. And in the duet "I Still Suits Me," as she sits on Paul Robeson's knee and chuckles with a suggestive look, the repressed sexuality of black women in Hollywood is released, if only for a few seconds.

When the producer David O. Selznick was casting *Gone With the Wind*, Hattie was the most versatile black actress working in Hollywood and the obvious candidate for the role of Scarlett O'Hara's mammy. In scene after scene she matches Vivien Leigh's spirited performance as the hot-tempered Southern belle, infusing the role with her own style of broad comedy and quiet dignity. As Hattie herself said: "I tried to make her a living, breathing character . . . to glorify Negro womanhood; not the modern, streamlined type of Negro woman who attends teas and concerts in ermine and mink, but the type of Negro of the period who gave us Harriet Tubman, Sojourner Truth and Charity Still."[5] In the comedy scenes audiences laugh with her, not at her, recognizing that she is in charge and will always have the last word, almost as if she were trying to reverse the slave-mistress roles. In her final scene she has a rare opportunity to parade her ability as a dramatic actress. When she tearfully describes to Melanie (Olivia de Havilland) the tragedy surrounding the death of Scarlett and Rhett's young daughter, the bossy, cantankerous mammy unexpectedly reveals deeper emotions. Her expression of pain and grief is very moving: rarely in Hollywood films did black actresses have the opportunity to show an emotional range, and here Hattie reveals that she can do much more in her roles than play the clown. Said Helen Taylor: "Her extended semi-monologue as she climbs the stairs with Melanie . . . affords the actress the opportunity to display a tragic depth, and melodramatic range which none of her other 'maid' roles allowed."[6]

In spite of her efforts, for some African Americans Hattie's presence in the movies was an embarrassment. The *Pittsburgh Courier*, a weekly black newspaper, denounced *Gone With the Wind* for presenting its black characters as "happy house servants and unthinking, hapless clods."[7] And during the Second World War, several black film celebrities, including Hattie, were criticized for perpetuating racist stereotypes. Walter White, executive secretary for the National Association for the Advancement of Colored People (NAACP), collected complaints from black men in the forces, one of whom accused Hattie and other black actors of lowering the morale of black soldiers, making "them wish that they were sometimes never even born. . . . I don't like to see my people act as though they were just in America to take up space."[8] A wartime poll published in *Negro Digest* revealed that while 53 percent of whites believed that films were fair to black people, 93 percent of the black people questioned thought otherwise.[9] Though not politically active like contemporaries such as Paul Robeson and Lena Horne, Hattie responded to her critics, in particular Walter White, by proclaiming that she would rather play a maid than be one: "What do you want me to do? Play a glamour girl and sit on Clark Gable's knee? When you ask me not to play the parts, what have you got to offer in return?"[10] In 1947, in an article in the *Hollywood Reporter*, she said: "I have never apologized for the roles I play. . . . I have been told that I have kept alive the stereotype of the Negro servant in the minds of theatre-goers. I believe my critics think the public more naïve than it actually is. . . . Arthur Treacher is indelibly stamped as a Hollywood butler, but I am sure no one would go to his home and expect him to meet them at the door with a napkin across his arm."[11]

Away from the studios, Hattie the person was far removed from the mammies she played on the screen. Lena Horne found this out when she arrived in Hollywood in 1942 and signed a contract with MGM. Lena was the first black artiste to sign a long-term movie contract—and enjoy financial security—but, after signing, she faced hostility from members of her own race. Black actors in Hollywood didn't trust her. They called her "an Eastern upstart" (because she had come from New York) and a tool of the NAACP. This culminated in a protest meeting at which the young singer was forced to get up and reassure her critics that she was not trying to start a revolt or to steal work from anyone. Lena later recalled in her autobiography:

Only one person among the Negro actors went out of her way to be understanding about the whole situation. That was Hattie McDaniel, who was, I suppose, the original stereotype of the Negro maid in the white public mind. Actually, she was an extremely gracious, intelligent, and gentle lady. She called me up and asked me to visit her. I went to her beautiful home and she explained how difficult it had been for Negroes in the movies, which helped give me some perspective on the whole situation. She was extremely realistic and had no misconception of the role she was allowed to play in the white movie world. She also told me she sympathized with my position and that she thought it was the right one if I chose it. I was very confused at the time; the one thing I had not expected was to get into trouble with my own race. Miss McDaniel's act of grace helped tide me over a very awkward and difficult moment and after that the public tension eased somewhat. But never completely. In a large part of the Hollywood Negro community I was never warmly received.[12]

By the mid-1940s, the roles Hattie played had become embarrassingly sentimental. For example, in Walt Disney's *Song of the South* (1946), she is reduced to the very thing she had spent years managing to subvert: a one-dimensional mammy caricature. Only one post–*Gone With the Wind* assignment offered her a brief departure from the stereotypes: as Minerva Clay, the soft-spoken mother of Parry, a law student wrongly accused of a murder in the Warner Brothers melodrama *In This Our Life* (1942), directed by John Huston. When her employer (Olivia de Havilland) visits her after the charge, the grief-stricken Minerva convinces her that Parry is innocent: "Police just come and took him off. . . . they don't listen to no colored boy," she says. The scene is not long (eighty seconds), but Hattie conveys real emotion. For her performance she was rewarded with a Best Acting citation from the National Board of Review.

After the war, Hattie discovered that winning an Oscar meant little. In 1948 David O. Selznick seemed to have forgotten her when he cast the small but important role of the kindly theatre dresser Clara Morgan in *Portrait of Jennie*. The role would have been perfect for Hattie, but Selznick gave it to Maude Simmons. With a movie career that had started to decline around 1946, the end came in 1949 with the release of *The Big Wheel* (a racing-car drama starring Mickey Rooney), which coincided with the release of five landmark films that attempted to take seriously America's "race" problem. These had no place for Hattie who, in the eyes of Hollywood, belonged to another era. The five films were *Home of the Brave*, *Lost Boundaries*, *Pinky*, *Intruder in the Dust*, and *No Way Out*, in which Sidney Poitier made a memorable screen debut. Hattie McDaniel died in 1952 as Poitier's star began to rise. Before the end of the decade he had become one of the first black actors to achieve star status in Hollywood, and the first to be nominated for a Best Actor Oscar (for *The Defiant Ones*, 1958).

Hattie's work has all too often been ignored by writers on film, including Marjorie Rosen in her exhaustive study of women in cinema: *Popcorn Venus: Women, Movies and the American Dream* (1973). In fact, Rosen ignored almost *all* African American women in the movies before the 1970s. Though she praises Diana Ross's "lovely and agonizing" portrait of Billie Holiday in *Lady Sings the Blues* (1972) and Cicely Tyson's "watchful, proud and loving mother" in *Sounder* (1972), there is no mention of Hattie, Louise Beavers, Ethel Waters, Lena Horne, Dorothy Dandridge, and the female members of the cast of the 1961 screen version of Lorraine Hansberry's *A Raisin in the Sun*: Claudia McNeil, Ruby Dee, and Diana Sands.

However, in the 1970s, the African American writer Donald Bogle *did* acknowledge the limitations imposed on Hattie while at the same time celebrating her success. Bogle described her as "one of the screen's greatest presences, a pre-Fellini-esque figure of the absurd and a marvel of energetic verve and enthusiasm."[13] Perhaps her appeal is best summed up by Eileen Landay in her book *Black Film Stars*: "As a fiercely protective, hard-to-please, devoted black mammy, she was the first to 'talk back,' thus defining herself as a human being. Although the standards she defended so fiercely were applied only to her masters and never to herself, although she seemed to have no life or desires other than to serve, the great talent and spirit of Hattie McDaniel overshadowed the parts written for her. Those who watched her knew that hidden behind the mammy was a real person."[14]

Notes

1. Harriet Beecher Stowe, *Uncle Tom's Cabin* (1853; Secaucus, N.J.: Longriver Press, 1976), 16–17.

2. Roland Flamini, *Scarlett, Rhett and a Cast of Thousands: The Filming of "Gone With the Wind"* (New York: Andre Deutsch, 1975), 184.

3. Danny Peary, *Cult Movie Stars* (New York: Simon and Schuster / Fireside, 1991), 49.

4. Donald Bogle, *Toms, Coons, Mulattoes, Mammies and Bucks: An Interpretive History of Blacks in American Films* (New York: Bantam Books, 1974), 118.

5. Carlton Jackson, *Hattie: The Life of Hattie McDaniel* (London: Madison Books, 1990), 62.

6. Helen Taylor, "The Mammy of Them All: *Gone with the Wind* and Race," in *Scarlett's Women: "Gone With the Wind" and Its Female Fans* (London: Virago Press, 1989), 173.

7. Stephen Bourne, "Denying Her Place: Hattie McDaniel's Surprising Acts," in *Women and Film: A Sight and Sound Reader*, Pam Cook and Philip Dodd, eds. (London: Scarlet Press, 1993), 31.

8. Bourne, "Denying Her Place," 31.

9. Bourne, "Denying Her Place," 31.

10. William J. Mann, "High-Hat Hattie: The Life of Movie Great Hattie McDaniel," *Frontiers*, March 17, 2000, 68.

11. Hattie McDaniel, "What Hollywood Means To Me," *Hollywood Reporter*, September 29, 1947.

12. Lena Horne with Richard Schickel, *Lena* (London: Andre Deutsch, 1966), 137–38.

13. Bogle, *Toms*, 115.

14. Eileen Landay, *Black Film Stars* (New York: Drake, 1973), 77.

~

CHAPTER FIVE

Swingin' the Dream

And every night I'd wait for her to come on stage and do her act. And it would just knock me completely out. Yes, she's a great little actress.

—Louis Armstrong,
The Louis Armstrong Companion: Eight Decades of Commentary

After completing work on *Gone With the Wind*, Butterfly returned to New York to appear in *Swingin' the Dream*, a Broadway musical described in *Time* (December 11, 1939) as a "lavish jitterbug extravaganza." Opening at Radio City's huge Center Theatre on November 29, 1939, this "swing" adaptation of William Shakespeare's *A Midsummer Night's Dream* used a racially integrated cast, rare at that time. In this show, set in New Orleans in 1890, at the time of the "birth of swing," the white cast members played the upper-class characters of Theseus's court, and the African American performers were cast as the artisans and wood fairies. The revels are staged for the benefit of Theseus, the governor of Louisiana, and the lovers wander into a voodoo forest, where they are placed under a spell by a cute black Puck, played by Butterfly, who works her magic with a flit gun. Unfortunately, no script for the show appears to have survived.

The white cast included Benny Goodman, and a young Dorothy McGuire, a few years before she became a Hollywood star in films like *Claudia*, *A Tree Grows in Brooklyn*, and *Gentleman's Agreement*. Perhaps the most famous name in a fantastic lineup of black artists was the legendary jazz musician Louis Armstrong as Bottom, dressed in a bright red fireman's uniform. He thoroughly enjoyed his Shakespearean debut. "Man," he said to the English jazz enthusiast Leonard Feather during the intermission on opening night, "if Old Shakespeare could see me now!"[1] In *Down Beat* magazine, the monthly "bible" of jazz music, Feather, fast becoming an influential jazz writer in the United States, naturally focused on Louis: "Armstrong . . . walks away with honors. From the moment he enters in the red fireman's suit as 'Bottom' and calls 'Peace, Brother,' until the final scene in which you learn Pyramus kicked the bucket, Louis is the same brilliant actor." But even he could not rescue the show. Feather spoke for many when he called the overambitious production a "hell of a fine nightmare."[2]

Maxine Sullivan, a popular jazz vocalist with a light and intimate style, played the part of Titania, queen of the fairies. "I guess that was because of the type of material I was doing," she later said.[3] Maxine had just enjoyed a big success with her swing version of the Scottish folk song "Loch Lomond," and "Darn That Dream," written especially for her to sing in the show by Eddie de Lange (lyrics) and Jimmy Van Heusen (music), went on to become a jazz standard. The rest of the cast included the comedienne Jackie "Moms" Mabley (Quince), Juano Hernandez (Oberon), ten years before he made his celebrated film appearance in MGM's *Intruder in the Dust*, Oscar Polk (Flute/Thisbe), who had just played Pork in *Gone With the Wind*, tap dancer Bill Bailey (Cupid), the Deep River Boys, and the singing and dancing Dandridge Sisters as three pixies who perform the title number. This act included a teenage Dorothy, who would later find fame in Hollywood. The musical also boasted around 120 musicians. Into this all-star mix came the ballet choreographer Agnes de Mille. She brought Whitey's Lindy Hoppers down from the World's Fair (and the Savoy Ballroom) for specialty numbers in the show. One of them, Norma Miller, later remarked on how difficult it was to perform on their excruciating schedule at the World's Fair and then attend rehearsals. It seems that Ms. de Mille was very demanding! Agnes de Mille would later have a great impact on the choreography of Broadway musicals in expanding the scope of dancing, especially with Rodgers and Hammerstein's *Oklahoma!* (1943) (its dream ballet started a trend), *Carousel* (1945), and *Brigadoon* (1947).

Donald Bogle notes that "during rehearsals, word spread among jazz aficionados and fans that *Swingin' the Dream* was a progressive production that made excellent use of its often underemployed Negro talents."[4] There were dazzling special effects: "The huge Center Theatre's stage was exploited for various trick and interesting effects, with sets and costumes modeled after Walt Disney's cartoons. Titania made an entrance in a World's Fair 'World of Tomorrow' electric wheelchair; a Murphy bed emerged from a tree in the forest; microphones (to help audibility in the cavernous playhouse) sprang up in the shape of caterpillars and snails; and there was a noteworthy scene of plantation life on the lawn of the governor's . . . mansion, with a cast of jitter-bugging celebrants."[5] Lionel Hampton, the black jazz musician and member of Benny Goodman's racially integrated band, wrote enthusiastically about the show and his high hopes for it in a column in the newspaper *Afro-American*. Bud Freeman, the leader of the show's other swing band, later recalled the show's promise:

> We were at Nick [Condon]'s for about six or seven weeks when we got an offer to do a Broadway show called *Swingin' the Dream*. The show was produced by Eric Charell, who had a tremendous success in Europe with a show called *White Horse Inn*. He came to America with enormous financial backing to create a revue mixing *Midsummer Night's Dream* with black vaudeville. He had just about the finest talent you could get. . . . If Charell had known the greatness of black people he could have had a revue that would still be running. There was some excellent music in the show. Jimmy Van Heusen wrote a number of pieces for it, and one of them, "Darn That Dream," has become a classic.[6]

It seems hard to believe that, in spite of the musical talents involved, the show failed to impress critics and attract an audience. The wealthy (white) writer and photographer Carl Van Vechten wrote to the African American poet Langston Hughes: "*Swingin' the Dream* was wonderful in spots. They made the mistake of making it too expensive. Benny Goodman, who wasn't needed at all, set them back $2,500 a week. Of course he played divinely and had several Negroes in his band including the old Small's drummer and Fletcher Henderson at the piano, but it interrupted the action."[7] Allen Woll comments: "Despite an excellent cast, most critics dismissed the new *Dream*," and he quotes the objections of the theatre critic John Chapman: "For foolish casting, take Louis Armstrong, dressed as a fireman and always carrying his trumpet, as Bottom. Or Maxine Sullivan, with a World's Fair Guide chair as her throne, as Titania. Butterfly McQueen as Puck, carrying a flit gun with which to charm her sleeping victims."[8] Chapman's views seem harsh, for the casting is inspired for a Broadway musical, especially in 1939, and even if the production was a shambles, surely the cast alone was worth seeing. But Allen Woll dismisses the show as "uninspired tomfoolery."[9] As described by Rosamond Gilder: "On the stage, Louis Armstrong blew his magic horn . . . jitterbugs danced madly, fantastic creatures cavorted and sang, masses of brilliant costumes deployed against gay or fantastic settings, in the orchestra pit and on either side bands provided swing in every mood and mode. Yet never once did all these elements come together or reach out to the spectator and make him take part, even vicariously, in the festivities."[10] In the *New York Times* (November 30, 1939), critic Brooks Atkinson praised Benny Goodman and his musicians, notably Lionel Hampton, but otherwise dismissed the show as a "hodge-podge of Shakespeariana" that failed to make good use of Shakespeare or its talented black cast members.[11]

One member of the opening night audience who was enthusiastic in his appraisal of the show was Leonard Feather. He later described the first performance as "remarkable" and recalled: "On either side of the stage, in mezzanine boxes, were two jazz groups that supplemented the Don Voorhees pit orchestra. One was the Benny Goodman Sextet . . . the other was Bud Freeman's Summa Cum Laude group. . . . this unique and delightful show received generally negative reviews. . . . All that remains of it is a song that still survives as a jazz standard, 'Darn That Dream.'"[12] Almost a decade later, Louis Armstrong remembered Butterfly, who made a big impression on her costar: "She's one of my favorite actresses. . . . And every night I'd wait for her to come on stage and do her act. And it would just knock me completely out. Yes, she's a great little actress."[13]

Swingin' the Dream closed on December 9 after only thirteen performances and reportedly at a loss of over $100,000. According to the *New York Times*, it was "one of the costliest failures of recent years."[14] Radio City's giant Center Theatre had to look beyond the legitimate theatre for amusements more suited to its vast size. Their search ended when the Hollywood skating star Sonja Henie took over the theatre for *It Happens on Ice* in October 1940. For Butterfly, hopes of a career on the Broadway stage were dashed. She had to wait thirty years before another opportunity came to appear in a production on the Great White Way. Regarding *Swingin' the Dream*, the musical theatre historian Ethan Mordden reflects in *Sing for Your Supper*, his study of Broadway musicals in the 1930s:

> *Swingin' the Dream* (1939) has to be one of the most fascinating bombs of all time. The last of the Center Theatre spectacles before the house went over to ice shows, *Swingin' the Dream* was a mixed-race jazzup of *A Midsummer Night's Dream*, with the Benny Goodman Sextette both onstage and in the pit, Louis Armstrong as Bottom, and Butterfly McQueen as Puck. (Instead of a magical flower, she employed a pump of her flit gun to enchant her victims.) The décor was in the style of Walt Disney, and, in the manner of the two jazzings of *The Mikado* earlier that year, the idea was to razz a classic with new art, especially jitterbug, swing, and anything else that might inflect Shakespeare with the flavor of now. For example, Titania (Maxine Sullivan) navigated the stage in a chair on wheels just like those at the World's Fair. The nobles were white (Dorothy McGuire played Helena) while the fairies and *Pyramus and*

Thisbe troupe were black. *The Great Waltz*'s Erik Charell produced, showing an astonishing comprehension of that American thirties show-biz obsession, the merging of art and pop. *Porgy and Bess* is its best-known example and *Swingin' the Dream* the least. It's hard to know what exactly went wrong, for even the critics, while disapproving, thought the dancing—the work of Agnes de Mille and Herbert White—was excellent.[15]

Notes

1. Leonard Feather, *From Satchmo to Miles* (London: Quartet Books, 1974), 20.

2. Laurence Bergreen, *Louis Armstrong: An Extravagant Life* (New York: Broadway Books, 1997), 411.

3. Sally Placksin, *Jazzwomen 1900 to the Present: Their Words, Lives and Music* (London: Pluto Press, 1985), 119.

4. Donald Bogle, *Dorothy Dandridge: A Biography* (New York: Amistad, 1997), 72.

5. Samuel Leiter, *Encyclopedia of the New York Stage 1930–40* (Westport, Conn.: Greenwood, 1989), 502.

6. Bud Freeman, *Crazeology: The Autobiography of a Chicago Jazzman* (Urbana: University of Illinois Press, 1989), 49–50.

7. Carl Van Vechten to Langston Hughes in *Remember Me to Harlem: The Letters of Langston Hughes and Carl Van Vechten, 1925–1964* by Langston Hughes, Carl Van Vechten, and Emily Bernard (New York: Alfred A. Knopf, 2001), 163.

8. Allen Woll, *Black Musical Theatre: From Coontown to Dreamgirls* (Baton Rouge and London: Louisiana State University Press, 1989), 184.

9. Woll, *Black Musical Theatre*, 184.

10. Rosamond Gilder in *Theatre Arts 2*, 1940, 93.

11. Bogle, *Dorothy Dandridge*, 72.

12. Leonard Feather, *The Jazz Years: Earwitness to an Era* (Cambridge, Mass.: Quartet Books, 1986), 59.

13. Joshua Berrett, ed., *The Louis Armstrong Companion: Eight Decades of Commentary* (New York: Schirmer Books, 1999), 132.

14. Bogle, *Dorothy Dandridge*, 73.

15. Ethan Mordden, *Sing for Your Supper: The Broadway Musical in the 1930s (Golden Age of the Broadway Musical)* (New York: Palgrave MacMillan, 2005), 201.

CHAPTER SIX

~

Butterfly in Hollywood

I didn't mind playing a maid the first time because I thought that was how you got into the business. But after I did the same thing over and over, I resented it. I didn't mind being funny, but I didn't like being stupid.

—Butterfly McQueen

On her return to Hollywood after *Swingin' the Dream*, Butterfly was reunited with her *Gone With the Wind* costar, Hattie McDaniel, for a Warner Brothers comedy called *Affectionately Yours* (1941). It starred Merle Oberon, Dennis Morgan, and Rita Hayworth. It was not a success. Clive Hirschhorn, in *The Warner Bros. Story*, summarizes what everyone felt about the film: "a dismal and dispiriting comedy about an ace newspaper reporter's efforts to woo back his ex-wife . . . it was a screwball comedy that misfired."[1] According to David Shipman in *The Great Movie Stars: The Golden Years*, the film was destined originally for Bette Davis, but Warner Brothers were seriously considering Merle as her successor, and gave the part to her.[2] It was a mistake, for Merle received some of the worst reviews of her film career. Said *Variety*: "[She] seems unequal to the task of essaying a type of role so skillfully handled in the past several years by Carole Lombard and more lately by Rosalind Russell."[3] Unsurprisingly, Merle and Warner Brothers ended their association after the failure of this disappointing production.

As a comedy actress, Merle was out of her depth and unable to deliver the goods, but *Affectionately Yours* did have Hattie McDaniel and Butterfly

McQueen to provide some bright moments, which the film desperately needed. They were cast in supporting roles as Cynthia and Butterfly, a couple of domestics in Merle's household. While Cynthia is tough, bossy, and cantankerous, Butterfly is nervous and delicate, and dissolves into floods of tears at the slightest provocation. Says Mel Watkins: "[Butterfly] played a tear-eyed maid who quaked at the slightest mishap, real or imagined. Skittish and fragile, her presence served to exaggerate McDaniel's bombast and aggressiveness."[4] Cynthia and Butterfly are devoted to their mistress and distressed at the breakup of their employer's marriage, but the two characters lack substance and often lapse into racial stereotype. However, it has been noted that Hattie's characterization almost turned the stereotype on its head. Says Mel Watkins: "Her role was contrasted with Butterfly McQueen's fumbling, whimpering domestic and assumed even greater comic impact. In one scene, after Merle Oberon gives instructions about where guests are to be seated for dinner and leaves the room, McDaniel, who disapproves of both the arrangements and her employer's new beau, turns to the equally unhappy McQueen and says, 'We gwine take dem plates over dere and put 'em over here and I'm gon' break 'em one by one over his head.' In this film McDaniel behaves like the actual mistress of the household."[5]

One of the most embarrassing scenes takes place in the middle of the night when a drunken Rickey Mayberry (Dennis Morgan), the estranged husband of Sue (Merle Oberon), arrives at her house and rings the doorbell. Cynthia and Butterfly are sharing a bed. On hearing the doorbell, Butterfly sits up and whines: "Who dat?" Cynthia stirs and asks: "Who dat say who dat?" Butterfly responds: "Who dat say who dat when I say who dat?" Donald Bogle says this might be the most demeaning line ever uttered by an African American actor in Hollywood cinema: "Her talents were often misused or misunderstood by directors and writers. In *Affectionately Yours*, she had to deliver what might be the most demeaning line ever uttered by a black in the movies. 'Who dat say who dat when you say dat,' she crooned. 'I never thought I would have to say a line like that,' the actress later said, obviously embarrassed. 'I had imagined that since I was an intelligent woman, I could play any kind of role.'"[6] Bogle adds that, from the cast, it was Butterfly who was singled out and praised by the critics: "Perhaps the final irony of that line and the best tribute to Butterfly McQueen's comic talent was that her performance in *Affectionately Yours* was thoroughly disarming and considered by some critics the best in the movie. '[The] only glints of brightness . . . are contributed by a hair-spring brownie called Butterfly McQueen, as a maid. Her frequent dissolves into tears upon the slightest provocation are ludicrous,' wrote *The New York Times*."[7]

When it was announced that MGM would make a film version of the black Broadway musical fantasy *Cabin in the Sky* (1940), there was disapproval from all sides. White studio executives were apprehensive, fearing such a venture would not make money, and the black press was concerned that the film would perpetuate racial stereotypes. In press interviews, the film's producer, Arthur Freed, tried to allay such fears: "I will spare nothing and will put everything behind it. It will be a picture on a par with any major film under the MGM banner."[8] On *Cabin*, Freed gave the Broadway director Vincente Minnelli his first feature assignment. Minnelli had a reputation for taste and style and he planned to approach the subject "with great affection rather than condescension. . . . A portion of the militant black and liberal white press was highly critical of the proposed endeavor, finding the story patronizing. But there were an equal number of publications supporting us. . . . We would never knowingly affront blacks . . . or anyone else for that matter."[9]

Filming commenced on *Cabin* in August 1942, with only Ethel Waters, recreating her magnificent performance as Petunia, and Rex Ingram, as Lucifer Junior, retained from the Broadway cast. Eddie "Rochester" Anderson (*Gone With the Wind*'s Uncle Peter) replaced Dooley Wilson as Little Joe. At that time, cinema audiences were more familiar with Rochester, who had been working in Hollywood since the early 1930s. He was best known for playing Jack Benny's valet-chauffeur Rochester van Jones on the radio and in comedy films. Wilson would eventually make his mark in Hollywood in 1943 as Sam, Humphrey Bogart's piano-playing sidekick, in *Casablanca*. The character of Georgia Brown, instead of being the dancing part that Katherine Dunham had played on Broadway, was revised as a singing role tailor-made for Lena Horne, who had just signed a long-term contract with MGM. Extra added attractions included jazz giants Louis Armstrong and Duke Ellington, dance innovator John "Bubbles" Sublett, the Hall Johnson Choir, and Butterfly as Lily, loyal friend and companion to Petunia. Also in the supporting cast were Oscar Polk and Ernest Whitman from *Gone With the Wind*.

In *The Films of Vincente Minnelli*, James Naremore acknowledges that the "excruciatingly condescending white versions" of Southern-black English are eliminated from the script, "an effect that becomes especially evident in the case of a minor player, Butterfly McQueen, who never uses the spacey sing-song that audiences (even audiences of films produced by blacks) had come to expect of her."[10] Naremore also acknowledges Minnelli's attempts to improve the look of the film, and to glamorize its female stars: "whenever Ethel Waters is seen in a bandanna, she wears fashionable earrings reminiscent of the Cartier jewelry she had sung about in *At Home Abroad* [the Broadway show from 1935, directed by Minnelli]; and when Lena Horne dresses up as a temptress, she exchanges her pillbox hat for a magnolia, pinning the visibly artificial blossom to her hair like Billie Holiday."[11]

Butterfly's appearance in *Cabin* is a departure from most of her other screen roles. In *Cabin* she isn't a maid, but a kind and supportive friend to the leading character, Petunia. She doesn't have a lot to do. All of her appearances are with the stars of the film, Ethel and "Rochester," and it's refreshing to see Butterfly without a maid's uniform. In *Cabin* she dresses smartly when attending the local church with Petunia, and there's no bandanna on her head when she appears in Petunia's home. The great Ethel Waters has several memorable songs, including "Taking a Chance on Love" and "Cabin in the Sky," both retained from the Broadway show, and "Happiness Is a Thing Called Joe," written specially for the film. Ethel also recorded a number with Butterfly and the Hall Johnson Choir: "Dat Suits Me," an African American spiritual. Sadly, this was not included in the final cut. Happily, in 1996, this lovely, gentle spiritual was heard for the first time when it was included in the superb CD of the original soundtrack. In fact, all the outtakes from the film were included, and in the comprehensive notes that accompany the CD, Marilee Bradford explains that "Dat Suits Me" preceded Petunia and Joe's picnic lunch when she sings "Cabin in the Sky": "Near the bend of a small river, a half dozen washerwomen are at work on the banks. Among them are Petunia and Lily, and all the women are singing the traditional 'Dat Suits Me.' The distant factory whistle blows at midday, signaling lunchtime, and Petunia runs off to prepare Joe's lunch." It is important to acknowledge that Bradford refers to the song in her notes as "Dat Suits Me," but Ethel, Butterfly, and the Hall Johnson Choir depart from the "Negro" dialect and sing "*That* suits me," a testament to their artistry and integrity. It is not made clear in the CD notes if the sequence was filmed and deleted, like one of Lena Horne's *Cabin* solos, "Ain't It the Truth." This was saved and later incorporated into an MGM short, *Studio Visit* (1946), and the compilation feature *That's Entertainment! III* (1994). For the record, Butterfly was rarely called upon to sing in her films, which is a pity, because her light, lilting voice is appealing. She should have been heard singing more often, but she can be heard crooning fragments of Stephen Foster's "My Old Kentucky Home" ("Jes a few mo' days to tote the weary load") in *Gone With the Wind* and the Negro spiritual "Sometimes I Feel Like a Motherless Child" in *Duel in the Sun* (1946). In later years she sang in two stage musicals: *The Athenian Touch* and *Curley McDimple* (see chapter 9) and her one-woman shows.

Lena Horne was looking forward to working with her close friend Vincente Minnelli. However, as she explained in her autobiography *Lena* (1966), she had been warned that Ethel Waters could be temperamental and tough on other singers. Lena acknowledged that Ethel had been "terribly exploited" and had become suspicious of everyone connected to the film, especially the studio bosses, but nothing could have prepared her for Ethel's outburst on the set of *Cabin*. Said Lena: "The atmosphere was very tense. . . . Miss Waters started to blow like a hurricane. It was an all-encompassing blow, touching everyone and everything that got in its way. Though I . . . may have been the immediate cause of it, it was actually directed at everything that had made her life miserable, the whole system that had held her back and exploited her."[12]

When *Cabin* was released, Ethel's fears were realized. It was their contract player Lena, not freelance Ethel, who MGM sent to New York to promote the film with Duke Ellington's band when they showcased it at the Capitol Theatre. The studio promoted Lena as the star of the film, not Ethel. Understandably Ethel barely mentions *Cabin* in her 1951 autobiography, other than to comment: "There was conflict between the studio and me from the beginning. . . . all through that picture there was so much snarling and scrapping that I don't know how in the world *Cabin in the Sky* ever stayed up there. I won all my battles on that picture. But like many other performers, I was to discover that winning arguments in Hollywood is costly. Six years were to pass before I could get another movie job."[13] The main beneficiaries of *Cabin*'s success were Lena, who went on to make another black cast musical success, *Stormy Weather*, for Twentieth Century Fox, as well as many guest appearances in popular MGM musical extravaganzas, and Vincente Minnelli. He went on to make a succession of wonderful films for MGM, including musical classics such as *Meet Me in St. Louis* (1944), *An American in Paris* (1951), and *Gigi* (1958), for which he received an Oscar for Best Director.

Ethel Waters was not the only cast member who was miserable on the set of *Cabin*. In an interview with Richard Lamparski in the 1960s, Butterfly's memories of *Cabin* were also unhappy ones. Lamparski says: "Rochester teased her unmercifully, Lena Horne treated her with contempt, and director Vincente Minnelli was nice to her face but cutting when she was not present."[14] Lena's "contempt" for Butterfly was also referred to in the first of the "booklets" Butterfly compiled and distributed to fans in the 1970s. In several pages of personal comments and observations (see appendix C), she describes an unpleasant incident that occurred during the taping of a wartime radio show, possibly *Jubilee* (May 13, 1944) (see chapter 8): "During one of our wars many actors in Hollywood voluntarily taped radio shows for the armed forces overseas. One day at the Hollywood and Vine CBS radio station we were given a ten minute break from a taping session. The glamorous, talented Lena Horne, finding herself alone, unseen and unheard by anyone but myself, looked me fully in the eye and with centuries of unleashed horridly bitter hatred called me 'You dog!' Thank you, Lena Horne, for introducing me to the stark, pitiable misery of a top success."[15] If Butterfly's version of the story is true, it is difficult to understand why Lena behaved so abusively towards her. James Gavin, Horne's biographer, comments:

> I've heard the story about Butterfly accusing Lena of calling her a dog. I wasn't there, so I can't swear it didn't happen. But it's the only story I've heard of Lena acting rudely towards anyone in the '40s. Lena was raised to carry herself with a high level of dignity, so she might have been offended by Butterfly's Tommish mannerisms. But she was also groomed to be a lady, and I can't imagine her insulting Butterfly so cruelly, at least not at that time. Does that make Butterfly an out-and-out liar? We'll never know. Might Butterfly have done something to provoke the "you dog!" outburst? We'll never know that either. Did Lena have a momentary meltdown? Did Butterfly hit a nerve in her? Totally possible.[16]

However, in an interview in 1973, when Butterfly was working at the Mount Morris Recreation Center–Marcus Garvey Park in New York, Lena spoke kindly and enthusiastically about her: "She's fantastic. Butterfly is sweet and bright, a very brilliant girl. She has always worked with young people uptown in Harlem. She never left her sources, she got treated very badly; but she has taught at schools up there, she has always concerned herself with the theatre. She is a giant."[17]

Butterfly found herself back at MGM—and under the direction of Vincente Minnelli again—for her next film assignment, the musical comedy *I Dood It* (1943). This frantic comedy was derived from a film that Buster Keaton had made for MGM titled *Spite Marriage* (1929), with many of the visual gags taken directly from that earlier film with almost no changes. It was partly rewritten to fit the slapstick and pantomime antics of comedy favorite Red Skelton, and partly a show musical built around Skelton's costar, tap dancer Eleanor Powell. She played Constance "Connie" Shaw, a star of Broadway musicals, who is idolized by a tailor's assistant, played by Skelton. The rather ungrammatical title was thought to have derived from one of Skelton's own catchphrases of the day, but instead it came from the song itself, "I Dood It! (If I Do, I Get a Whippin')," written especially for Skelton in 1942. In *Directed by Vincente Minnelli*, Stephen Harvey notes: "Producer Jack Cummings must have hoped that Minnelli could infuse this nonsense with a little style, but even visually *I Dood It* is indistinguishable from a dozen other Metro mediocrities of the day."[18]

In the musical interludes, Eleanor Powell's vaudevillian gymnastics were not Minnelli's forte. He was more at home with two glamorous guest stars,

Lena Horne and the Trinidadian pianist Hazel Scott, who performed a rousing Café Society version of the fall of Jericho. Minnelli barely acknowledges the film in his autobiography, describing it as a "comic potboiler" and explains that MGM "was stuck with footage and sets of a project that wasn't working."[19] He adds: "If nothing else, the picture taught me that I could function in an uninteresting exercise if I had to."[20] Minnelli also recalled a complaint he received from an outraged fan regarding a delightful scene in which Butterfly, in a minor supporting role as Powell's dresser Annette, encounters Red Skelton sitting on a park bench:

> He'd taken exception to the scene where Red, very confused about his predicament, is sitting on a park bench. Butterfly McQueen joins him. Her little black dog (played by Baba, my then pet poodle) sits on the other side. Red, in his bewilderment, first talks to Butterfly, then turns to talk to the dog. I thought it was a mildly amusing bit. "How dare you make fun of black people by equating them to a dog?" the moviegoer wrote. I was surprised by such an interpretation. Like my general attitude to the picture, this was the farthest thing from my mind. My thoughts were too filled with the carrot Arthur [Freed] was dangling before me in the form of our next project [*Meet Me in St. Louis*].[21]

In 1945 Republic Pictures celebrated its tenth anniversary by releasing a John Wayne feature called *Flame of the Barbary Coast*. Herbert Yates, Republic's founder and president, approved a budget for the film of $600,000, a huge sum for the studio. Joseph Kane, the noted B-film director of the popular Roy Rogers series, directed from a script by Borden Chase. The film is set in San Francisco and climaxes with the 1906 earthquake. Reviewers found the movie lavish, if a tale too often told. Wayne stars as Duke Fergus, a Montana cattleman, who falls for Ann "Flaxen" Tarry (Ann Dvorak), a beautiful dance-hall hostess. After losing his gambling winnings to a card cheat, Wayne takes some lessons from a professional gambler back home and sets out to get his money back. The original poster promised that the film would be "packed with the thrill and spectacle of the West's most exciting era!" Reviewers were unimpressed, though the movie did pick up a couple of Oscar nominations for Sound Recording and Scoring of a Dramatic or Comedy Picture. In a minor supporting role as Beulah, "Flaxen" Tarry's maid, Butterfly has one or two memorable scenes. She first appears looking disdainfully at her mistress who is bathing in a tub that has been built into the floor. "Bath tubs in the floor," Beulah remarks, unimpressed. Her brief remark reveals a familiarity between the two women that permits the black maid to voice her opinions. In the following scene, Beulah answers the door to Duke Fergus. "Miss Flaxen says she sees you naturally in a little while," says Beulah.

When Duke asks if he can use the telephone, Beulah responds: "Huh? Oh, that thing. You twist the handle once and someone says, 'This is the bar.'" Later, Beulah defiantly stands up to the film's villain, the casino owner Boss Tito Morell (Joseph Schildkraut). It was unusual for a black maid in a Hollywood movie to "talk back" to white characters, unless she was played by Hattie McDaniel. Beulah insists that he sees Miss Flaxen, but Morell replies: "I'll see her later." An irritated and unhappy Beulah responds: "That's what you told her *last* time!"

In 1939 MGM's *The Women* (see chapter 2) was unusual in that it had an all-female cast, but the African American actresses who appear in the film, all in bit roles, are barely visible. Apart from a brief appearance by Butterfly as Lulu, the cosmetics counter maid, if you blink you'll miss Theresa Harris as a dogkeeper, Hattie Noel as a maid on a train, and Florence O'Brien as a restroom maid. When Joan Crawford (as Crystal Allen) asks Lulu to go to her apartment and prepare a meal for her boyfriend, the wise-cracking Pat (Virginia Grey) quips: "She [Crystal] thinks because Lulu's dark he won't be able to see her." The same could be said about the characters played by Theresa, Hattie, and Florence.

The 1940s were a tough time for black actresses in Hollywood, and there were few openings for them in the movies. The 1940 United States census reports that of the 2,426 actors in Los Angeles, only 51 were black. Of the 910 male dancers, showmen, and athletes, a mere 33 were black. Of the 1,271 experienced actors in Hollywood, 42 were black. Of the 743 actresses working in the film capital, only a paltry 15 were African American.[22] Among those women were Butterfly, Hattie McDaniel and her sister Etta, Louise Beavers, Theresa Harris, Jeni Le Gon, and Lillian Yarbo. And yet, there were glimmers of change, especially during the war. In 1942, Lena Horne's seven-year contract with MGM was a breakthrough, and in 1943 she costarred with Ethel Waters in *Cabin in the Sky*, the first film to give a black female star (Waters) above-the-title billing. Others, who spent many years playing bit roles as maids, have never been given the credit they deserve. For example, from 1930 to 1958, Theresa Harris appeared in more than seventy films. She is best remembered for her role as Bette Davis's lively maid Zette in *Jezebel* (1938), but Theresa deserves a place in film history for portrayal of Alma, the servant girl in *I Walked With a Zombie* (1943), produced by Val Lewton and directed by Jacques Tourneur. Loosely based on Charlotte Brontë's *Jane Eyre*, the film is an atmospheric tale of voodoo and forbidden love in the Caribbean. Alma and another black character, the calypso singer played by Sir Lancelot, who acts as a "Greek chorus," stand out because they are humanized by Tourneur and do not speak in "Negro" dialect, rare for black actors in Hollywood films at that time. Tourneur later reflected in an unidentified interview, "I have always refused to caricature black people. I have never, or hardly ever, showed them in the role of servants. I have always endeavored to give them a profession, to have them speak normally rather than going for some comic effect. . . . I have often been accused of being a 'nigger lover' and for many months I was kept away from the studios for that very reason. It was a kind of grey list." Another example is the Christmas classic *It's a Wonderful Life* (1946), directed by Frank Capra, starring James Stewart, in which Lillian Randolph plays a maid but is very much a part of the family she works for. As Annie, Randolph speaks her mind to her employers, the Baileys, and it is impossible to imagine Ma Bailey (Beulah Bondi) treating her as anything less than an equal. Like Alma in *I Walked With a Zombie*, Annie is humanized, and beautifully integrated into the plot, but such examples are rare, and the black actresses in these films are always playing servants. Mostly the roles were one-dimensional stereotypes and were not happy experiences for the actresses who played them. When the jazz singer Billie Holiday went to Hollywood in 1947 to make a movie, *New Orleans*, she thought she was going to play herself in it and sing a few songs in a nightclub setting. She felt humiliated when she discovered she had to play a stereotypical maid. For actresses like Butterfly, it was play maids or starve, and even directors, like Jacques Tourneur, were vulnerable and risked unemployment if they questioned or challenged the status quo.

To summarize, the African American film scholar Michele Wallace has noted that Butterfly's "now infamous" scene in *Gone With the Wind* in which she admits to knowing nothing 'bout birthin' babies "made black women cringe for the next 50 years":

> Although their work was always first rate and, at the very least, highly entertaining, black performers such as McQueen, Hattie McDaniel and Stepin Fetchit have had no end of castigation, ostracism, and condemnation for their stereotypical roles in white supremacist films of the 30s and 40s. . . . When I first saw McQueen in *Cabin in the Sky*, she instantly became one of my favorite actresses. . . . In *Cabin*, the subtle way McQueen plays dimwit to Ethel Waters's hot mama reminds me of one of those old Gracie Allen and George Burns routines. But McQueen never got the work nor the credit she deserved. Moreover, black actresses of yore have often been considered unworthy of note. Since they were just a bunch of Mammies, Jezebels, and Tragic Mulattoes, the conventional wisdom goes, why honor them? But how about honoring what they were able to do with what they had? . . . McQueen's stand on not accepting denigrating roles is well documented although usually forgotten. It kept her out of work most of her career. . . . I remember her best from the '70s as I walked to classes at City College on Convent Avenue, sweeping the walk of what I thought was her house.[23]

Notes

1. Clive Hirschhorn, *The Warner Bros. Story* (London: Octopus, 1979), 229.

2. David Shipman, *The Great Movie Stars: The Golden Years* (London: Hamlyn, 1970), 417.

3. Undated review, quoted in James Robert Parish and Don E. Stanke, *The Glamour Girls* (Carlstadt, N.J.: Rainbow Books, 1975), 625.

4. Mel Watkins, *On the Real Side: A History of African American Comedy from Slavery to Chris Rock*, rev. ed. (New York: Simon and Schuster, 1999), 242.

5. Watkins, *On the Real Side*, 238–39.

6. Donald Bogle, *Toms, Coons, Mulattoes, Mammies and Bucks: An Interpretive History of Blacks in American Films* (New York: Bantam Books, 1974), 129–30. The quotation from Butterfly in this extract was taken from her interview in the *New York Times* (July 21, 1968).

7. Bogle, *Toms*, 129–30.

8. Hugh Fordin, *The World of Entertainment! Hollywood's Greatest Musicals* (New York: Doubleday, 1975), 71.

9. Vincente Minnelli with Hector Arce, *I Remember It Well* (London: Angus and Robertson, 1975), 121.

10. James Naremore, *The Films of Vincente Minnelli* (Cambridge: Cambridge University Press, 1993), 67.

11. Naremore, *Films*, 67.

12. Lena Horne with Richard Schickel, *Lena* (London: Deutsch, 1966), 154. For further information, see Stephen Bourne, *Ethel Waters: Stormy Weather* (Lanham, Md.: Scarecrow Press, 2007), 51–54.

13. Ethel Waters with Charles Samuels, *His Eye Is on the Sparrow* (London: W. H. Allen, 1951; New York: Da Capo, 1992), 258.

14. Richard Lamparski, *Whatever Became Of?* vol. 2 (New York: Ace Books, 1967), 37–38.

15. Butterfly McQueen, *Miscellanea 1* (see appendix C).

16. James Gavin, by e-mail, April 5, 2007.

17. R. Couri Hay, "Lena!" *Andy Warhol's Interview*, January 1973, 20.

18. Stephen Harvey, *Directed by Vincente Minnelli* (New York: Museum of Modern Art / Harper and Row, 1989), 45.

19. Minnelli with Arce, *I Remember*, 127.

20. Minnelli with Arce, *I Remember*, 127.

21. Minnelli with Arce, *I Remember*, 127–28.

22. Donald Bogle, *Dorothy Dandridge: A Biography* (New York: Amistad, 1997), 93–94.

23. Michele Wallace, "Invisibility Blues: When Dream Girls Grow Old," *Village Voice*, January 30, 1996, 21.

CHAPTER SEVEN

~

Mildred Pierce

From the vantage point of individual talent or from the perspective of the limitations of the "star" system, despite the obvious stereotyping, Butterfly McQueen obviously made a unique contribution to American film. In fact, she belonged, as well, to a complex tradition of feisty maids and housekeepers (most of them white working-class types) in film noir that deserves further study.

—Michele Wallace, *Dark Designs and Visual Culture*

After Prissy in *Gone With the Wind*, Butterfly's role as Joan Crawford's maid Lottie in Warner Brothers' *Mildred Pierce* (1945), directed by Michael Curtiz, is her most controversial. In Albert J. LaValley's introduction to the screenplay of *Mildred Pierce*, published in the Wisconsin/Warner Bros. Screenplay Series in 1980, he acknowledges that Butterfly gives "a rich comic performance as Mildred's maid, animating an empty part with her high voice and much business. Curtiz must have seen that the movie could use some comic relief," but he adds that "unfortunately much of the humor has racist overtones, and McQueen herself gets no screen credit."[1] The "racist overtones" will be explored in this chapter, but it seems incredible that Butterfly's name was missing from the list of actors in the opening credits. By 1945, though her screen appearances had been rare, she was firmly established in Hollywood as a supporting player and, with the exception of *The Women*, her name had been included in all of the opening credits of her previous movies.

Mildred Pierce is one of Butterfly's best-known films. It was also the second film in which she appeared to be nominated for an Oscar for Best Film and to receive an Oscar for Best Actress (Joan Crawford). In addition to being a cult *and* camp classic, *Mildred Pierce* is also a highly regarded melodramatic film noir, based upon a 1941 James M. Cain novel. Joan Crawford plays the title role, a lower-class California divorcée with two young daughters to support. The older daughter, Veda (Ann Blyth), is vain and selfish. The younger, Kay (Jo Ann Marlowe), is Veda's opposite: a carefree, fun-loving tomboy. At first, Mildred supports her daughters by taking a job as a waitress and in her spare time baking cakes and making pies for their neighbors. As Lottie, Butterfly is first seen helping Mildred make cakes and pies. Eventually Mildred opens her own restaurant and becomes a successful businesswoman, but she finds herself competing with Veda for the affections of her second husband, who is then found murdered. As Mildred climbs the social ladder from lower-class housewife to successful businesswoman, by the end of the film, Lottie has graduated from helping Mildred in her kitchen to becoming her full-time maid in her grand mansion.

In addition to being a first-class murder mystery, *Mildred Pierce* is a typical "woman's film" of the 1940s, a melodrama in which a woman's anguish is at the centre, aimed at an audience of women because the star of the film, Joan Crawford, mainly appealed to them. By 1942, with eleven million men in uniform, a great percentage of the cinema-going public in wartime America were women. Hollywood movies began to focus on their problems and emotions, as well as female companionship, but few films showed American women in factories or in uniform. Films were more concerned with a woman's search for happiness, self-sacrifice, or the problems of a beautiful woman in love with a married man. Few women were shown as emancipated, fighting for a safe and secure world. The few exceptions included *So Proudly We Hail* (1943) and *Cry Havoc* (1943), both of which focused on U.S. Army nurses based in Bataan in the Philippines. David O. Selznick's *Since You Went Away* (1944) concentrated on a mother and her two daughters on the American home front. Hollywood films of this time gave no credibility to what women were doing in wartime. After the war ended, American women were no longer expected to seek an escape from reality, and as men returned home from the war, box office—and social—demands changed.

During the war, Hollywood studios recognized the potential box office appeal in "women's films," but it was MGM and Warner Brothers that really capitalized on the genre. In fact, Warner Brothers fared best for they had such stars as Bette Davis (from 1932) and Joan Crawford (from 1943) under contract. Both Davis and Crawford had enjoyed long careers in the movies, and they knew what kind of scripts to look for. Before joining Warner Brothers in 1943, Crawford had been under contract to MGM for eighteen years, taking starring roles in some very popular melodramas, influencing women's tastes in fashion, and leading a very public private life, as reported in fan magazines. During the war, MGM lost interest in her. The studio preferred to elevate newer, younger glamorous stars, such as Lana Turner and Hedy Lamarr. Says Lawrence J. Quirk in *The Films of Joan Crawford*: "For two years after leaving MGM she did not work. In 1943 she had signed a contract with Warner Brothers for a third of what MGM had paid her, but she could not find a script that satisfied her and asked to be taken off salary. . . . producer Jerry Wald, then at Warners, found *Mildred Pierce*. As soon as Crawford read the script she knew it was right for her. . . . The role of Mildred had depth and dimension and under Michael Curtiz's direction Miss Crawford gave a technically expert and fully realized interpretation that won her the 1945 Academy Award and restored her to stardom."[2]

Women viewing the film in 1945 would have said that Joan Crawford had "succeeded" in the film, but it was a success only in terms of her performance, for example, receiving the Academy Award "Oscar" for Best Actress and reviving her film career. But Mildred is punished throughout the melodrama for what she does. She does not "succeed" at the end of the story. Throughout the film, Mildred has an awful life, but all she really wants to do are the things that men do and get credit for, but *because she is a woman* Mildred has to pay, and she pays dearly, in emotional suffering, and not necessarily as a result of the loss of her business, or Veda's cruel treatment of her, or even the tragic death of her young daughter, Kay. Mildred is punished in terms of failed relationships. Everything that Mildred does, which takes her out of the traditional female role, leads to punishment of one kind or another. She aims to do what men do, and pays dearly for it. In her essay "*Mildred Pierce* and Women in Film," June Sochen says the film "ended the playful admiration of the Independent Woman. She was too dangerous, too suggestive of new, unexpected possibilities. If Mildred had succeeded both personally and in the business world she would have created a new social type: a career wife-mother . . . precisely at the time when American society wanted to return to normalcy. . . . Mildred Pierce had to be destroyed to eliminate any troublesome thoughts held by working mothers. . . . Mildred Pierce had to go home again. In the Depression thirties, a divorced housewife in business may have been portrayed as heroic; in 1945, she had to be reminded of her proper role."[3] However, Molly Haskell argues that what the audience remembers is the independence, not the downfall or humiliation of the heroine: "We remember . . . Joan Crawford looking about as wobbly as the Statue of Liberty."[4]

Ironically, in spite of the success of *Mildred Pierce* and the Oscar she won for her memorable performance, Joan Crawford eventually found herself out of work. She made her final film in 1970 while some of her male contemporaries, including Henry Fonda, James Stewart, and John Wayne, continued playing leading roles. Towards the end of her life (she died in 1977) Crawford complained: "Today there are no jobs. I wish I were Duke Wayne. Everything that I have was all given to me by the motion picture industry. I was born in front of a camera. I don't know anything else."

There is no sympathy shown for *any* of the female characters in *Mildred Pierce* except, perhaps, Butterfly's Lottie. Apart from Mildred, who is not spared *anything*, Veda Pierce becomes a murderess; Kay Pierce—one of the film's most delightful characters—dies of pneumonia early on in the story; and Ida (Eve Arden), the restaurant hostess who befriends Mildred, is either a sexually frustrated spinster or, according to Richard Barrios, "cryptolesbian," "neither requiring nor desiring undue male attention."[5] There was no place for a fully rounded, openly lesbian character in a Hollywood movie in 1945.

Butterfly's character, Lottie, stands out because she seems happy throughout, and enjoys a friendly relationship with her employer, but she does not socialize with any of the white characters. In this respect, Lottie conforms to a Hollywood racial stereotype. She is only seen in a domestic role, in the kitchens of Mildred's home and restaurant, with a broom in her hand, or answering the door in a maid's uniform. And yet, from start to finish, a warmth and familiarity between the two women can be found. Mildred is Lottie's boss, but Lottie refers to her as "Mrs. Pierce," *not* "Miss Mildred," which was the custom for Hollywood's black movie maids. Throughout the film, there is camaraderie between the two women suggesting that Mildred relates to Lottie because they are both from the lower classes. Though it is not stated, it is clear that Mildred could have employed a more experienced and competent maid, but she keeps Lottie employed, right to the end of the story. Mildred treats Lottie with respect.

Early in the film, Mildred is too proud to let Veda know she has taken a job as a waitress to earn a living, but Veda is sly and uncovers the truth. When she finds her mother's waitress uniform, she gives it to Lottie and makes her wear it. "Where did you get that uniform?" Mildred asks Lottie. She replies: "Miss Veda gave it to me. She makes me wear it in case I have to answer the doorbell. She hollered, and went on, so I put it on just to keep her quiet." It is important to acknowledge how Butterfly delivers the following line: "She makes me wear it in case I have to answer the doorbell." She says it dismissively, suggesting that in Mildred's home, she is treated as one of the family, except by Veda, who uses Lottie—and the uniform—to expose and upset her mother.

On the opening night of Mildred's restaurant, Lottie is integrated with the white kitchen staff and can be seen "pitching in" with Mildred, Ida, and Wally Fay (Jack Carson) to make the night a success. In a lighthearted moment, when Mildred ties a white apron around Wally's waist, Lottie pipes up: "You look very pretty Mr. Fay!" and Wally does a double take. In the same scene, Lottie tells everyone: "This is just like my wedding night. *So* exciting." For the first—and last—time in a Hollywood movie, Butterfly is given a husband, though he doesn't have a name, and exists off-screen. In most of her movie roles, Butterfly was "on the shelf," thus conforming to Hollywood's depiction of black women as asexual and comedic. In *Cabin in the Sky* there was no man in her life, only her friendship with Petunia, and religion; in *I Dood It* she tells Red Skelton a story about a "wandering minstrel" who "strolled right in, and then strolled right out" of her life; and in *Duel in the Sun* (see chapter 8), she is isolated on a Texas ranch in the middle of nowhere and can only dream of marrying.

Mildred and Lottie have the highest regard for each other. When Mildred returns home after a long vacation, she greets Lottie, whose face lights up with pleasure and who exclaims: "This is a day for rejoicing, it certainly is!" Lottie's familiarity with the Pierce family continues, even after she has been "promoted" to being a maid, with her *own* uniform, in Mildred's lavish mansion. When Mildred's ex-husband, Bert Pierce (Bruce Bennett), visits, Lottie dispenses with formalities and tells him, offhandedly, that Mrs. Pierce is "in there," waving her hand towards a downstairs room. Quickly correcting herself, she adds: "I mean, this way please." Finally, in her last scene in the film, Veda's birthday party, Lottie exclaims to Jack, the haughty, elderly white butler (Jack Mower): "Jack, isn't this a beautiful night? I just *love* parties, don't you?" Surprised at being addressed by Lottie, Jack looks down his nose and replies, "I beg your pardon?" Lottie, realizing her error, says simply, and charmingly, "Thank you kindly."

The screenplay is credited to Ranald MacDougall, who was nominated for an Oscar, but Albert J. LaValley notes that various writers made contributions to the script. They included William Faulkner, one of the twentieth century's most acclaimed novelists and winner of the 1949 Nobel Prize for Literature. Born in New Albany, Mississippi, in the American South, Faulkner confronted racism in rural Mississippi in the 1940s in his novel *Intruder in the Dust* (1948). Lottie is not black in James M. Cain's novel; it was Faulkner who changed her into a black woman. However, LaValley says he did not envision Butterfly McQueen. Faulkner's Lottie is more stereotypical, a Hollywood mammy like Hattie McDaniel, "a Dilsey type [from Faulkner's novel *The Sound and the Fury*], who finally comforts a distraught Mildred after Kay's death by holding her and singing 'Steal Away.' 'God damn! How's that for a scene?' Faulkner wrote in the margin."[6]

Joan Crawford was probably the most genuinely soulful star actress in the Golden Age of Hollywood, with disappointments, angers, and destroyed illusions in between her career triumphs. You can see it in her eyes, her mouth, her walk, and her voice. In real life and in her early film melodramas, she came from white trash: disregarded, laughed at, pitied. She could almost be an honorary African American. Then, from the garbage, comes Joan's inner dragon and, boy, does she *roar!* Don't mess with me, fellas! The *real* racism is that no *Mildred Pierce* type of Hollywood film has ever been made starring an African American leading lady, and still isn't today. In 1975 there was *Mahogany*, starring Diana Ross, a hugely entertaining, glossy soap opera, set in the world of fashion, but this was an exception. Today, the likes of Angela Bassett and Halle Berry are *not* starring in the equivalents of the melodramas Joan Crawford made in the 1940s. What a waste. Oscar winner Halle Berry could be great in a remake of a Crawford classic, like *Mildred Pierce*, *Humoresque*, or *Sudden Fear* . . . if only Hollywood would let her.

Notes

1. Albert J. LaValley, *Mildred Pierce* (Madison: University of Wisconsin Press, 1980), 45.

2. Lawrence J. Quirk, *The Films of Joan Crawford* (New York: Citadel Press, 1968), 20.

3. June Sochen, "*Mildred Pierce* and Women in Film," *American Quarterly* 30, no. 1 (Spring 1978), 13.

4. Molly Haskell, *From Reverence to Rape: The Treatment of Women in the Movies* (New York: Holt, Rinehart, 1974), 49.

5. Richard Barrios, *Screened Out: Playing Gay in Hollywood from Edison to Stonewall* (New York: Routledge, 2003), 214.

6. LaValley, *Mildred Pierce*, 35–36.

CHAPTER EIGHT

~

Making a Stand

It is to be hoped that her courageous stand will have some effect on Hollywood opinion, and in encouraging Negro rebels. And in any case, one must applaud her strength of character in taking such a decision for her principles.

—Peter Noble, *The Negro in Films*

The more sinister aspect of this period . . . is reflected in the case of Butterfly McQueen, an actress of great promise who practically never found work in Hollywood after her protest in 1946 against the comic maid roles into which she was regularly cast.

—David Robinson, *Financial Times* (London)

In the 1940s, in between her film assignments, Butterfly made a number of appearances on American radio shows including *Jubilee* (1943–1945), *The Jack Benny Program* (1943–1944), *Birds Eye Open House* (1944) with Dinah Shore, and *The Danny Kaye Show* (1945–1946). Her experiences on these shows varied. In 1944, unhappy with the role she was playing, Butterfly terminated her contract with the Jack Benny series, but it is not generally known that her role in the Danny Kaye series was praised for departing from the usual stereotype.

Jubilee was a variety show with a predominantly black cast that was taped in Hollywood for the AFRS (Armed Forces Radio Services). These shows were then broadcast to men and women serving in the armed forces overseas. Regulars in the cast included the Master of Ceremonies, actor Ernie "Bubbles" Whitman, who had played the carpetbagger's friend in *Gone With the Wind*, and Butterfly, who provided comedy relief in various sketches. Throughout the series, musical interludes featured such guest artistes as Bill Robinson, the Delta Rhythm Boys, Lena Horne, Ella Fitzgerald, Thelma Carpenter, and the orchestras of Jimmy Lunceford, Count Basie, and Fletcher Henderson. A review in the *California Eagle* notes that Butterfly "borrowed for the occasion from the Jack Benny show . . . exchanged a cross-fire barrage of gags [with Ernest Whitman] that had the guys and gals in the audience going into convulsions."[1]

Surviving programs reveal that poor Butterfly participated in comedy sketches that mostly made her the butt of the joke. In an edition of *Jubilee*, recorded in August 1943, Eddie "Rochester" Anderson makes a guest appearance and subjects Butterfly to jokes that, sixty years on, make for uncomfortable listening. After performing "Life's Full of Consequences" from the recently released *Cabin in the Sky*, gravel-voiced Rochester tells Ernie he is in a hurry, but he is prevented from leaving when Butterfly joins them and makes a play for him. Rochester reminds Ernie he is in a *terrible* hurry when Ernie informs him she is "a little man crazy." "Maybe," replies Rochester, "but I ain't a little man!" After she introduces herself to Rochester: "Yes, I'm Butterfly," Rochester responds: "Butterfly? When are you gonna crawl out of your cocoon?" The audience roars with laughter. Butterfly tells Rochester he is her "great big beautiful dream man. Let me snuggle up close to you." Rochester responds: "Get away from me, moth. I ain't your flame!" The rest of the sketch continues in this way, with Rochester ridiculing Butterfly, referring to her as a "brother" and a freak with six toes. Here is an extract:

BUTTERFLY: "Don't you remember me, Rochester? We met at a party last month."
ROCHESTER: "Where?"
BUTTERFLY: "On Central Avenue. Don't you remember the petite, vivacious, charming little girl at the party?"
ROCHESTER: "Oh, yeah."
BUTTERFLY: "Well, I'm related to her. . . . What do you think of me?"
ROCHESTER: "Well, you ain't no Lena Horne!"
BUTTERFLY: "Lena Horne? What has she got what I haven't got?"
ROCHESTER: "Oh, come now [audience roars with laughter]. Besides, brother, it ain't what, it's where!"
BUTTERFLY: "Well, gee, don't you think I have nice eyes?"
ROCHESTER: "No."
BUTTERFLY: "Don't you think I have pretty teeth?"

ROCHESTER: "No."
BUTTERFLY: "Don't you think I have a charming personality?"
ROCHESTER: "No."
BUTTERFLY: "You don't like very much about me, do you?"
ROCHESTER: "Sure I do. It ain't every girl who's got six toes" [audience roars with laughter].
BUTTERFLY: "Oh, well. You might change your mind after you get to know me better. Let's make a date. How about Thursday night?"
ROCHESTER: "No."
BUTTERFLY: "Friday night?"
ROCHESTER: "No."
BUTTERFLY: "Saturday night?"
ROCHESTER: "Oh, definitely not. . . . Well, I gotta go along now. So long."
BUTTERFLY: "I'll go with you, Rochester."
ROCHESTER: "You can't go with me, gal. I'm going to an army camp, there's nothing but men there. What would you do in a camp with a couple of thousand men?"
BUTTERFLY: "Oh, come now!" [audience roars with laughter].[2]

Butterfly may be given the last word (or joke) in this sketch, but it comes after she has been subjected to what amounts to nothing more than a humiliating torrent of abuse from Rochester. The sketch isn't funny at all, it's deeply offensive.

Similarly, in a later edition of *Jubilee*, recorded on June 26, 1944, Butterfly allows herself to be subjected to jokes that play on her movie image as simple-minded and stupid. Butterfly reminds Ernie Whitman that he promised to introduce her to the show's guest artiste, the popular Portuguese-Brazilian samba singer and film star Carmen Miranda. On meeting Butterfly, Carmen says something in Portuguese to which Butterfly responds: "I'm awfully sorry, Miss Miranda, but I don't speak French." Carmen explains: "In Brazil, where I was born, they speak nothing but Portuguese." Butterfly pipes up: "Gee, I'm glad I wasn't born there, I wouldn't understand a word anyone was saying. . . . I've been waiting to meet you for ever so long. I can hardly believe it's true. Here we are at last, face to face, the Brazilian Bombshell and the Central Avenue dud."[3] One can only assume that Butterfly's desire to support the war effort, and to entertain the troops, led to her agreement to take part in these sketches.

In 1943–1944, Butterfly was featured in *The Jack Benny Program*, one of America's most successful radio shows, starring Jack Benny, one of the country's most popular comedians. From 1932 he became one of the biggest stars in classic American radio. Eddie "Rochester" Anderson had been playing Benny's valet-chauffeur, Rochester van Jones, in the series since

1938. Rochester proved to be as popular with audiences as Benny, and they remained a favorite double-act in American comedy on radio, on television, and in films until 1965. Regulars in the show also included Mary Livingstone as Benny's wise-cracking girlfriend. Butterfly joined the series in 1943 as Rochester's girlfriend, but the actress quit the show when she was requested to play Mary Livingstone's maid. Butterfly decided to make a stand because she felt her maid's role was a negative reflection of African American women. She later explained: "The late Jack Benny once wrote me into a life-time contract—one of his own making. When I wanted to leave his show I just took my contract to my radio union and presto-change-o—I was free. I said I left because I was switched from occasionally playing Rochester's girlfriend to being Mary Livingston's maid."[4]

Following her disappointment with the Jack Benny program, Butterfly joined the singer Dinah Shore in *Birds Eye Open House*. The *Chicago Defender* noted that Butterfly "shines on the Dinah Shore program."[5] There followed a regular role in *The Danny Kaye Show* for CBS. This series also featured Eve Arden, Lionel Stander, and bandleader Harry James, as well as occasional guests, such as Sophie Tucker, Betty Hutton, Carmen Miranda, and Orson Welles. Despite its clever writing by the radio legend Goodman Ace, Kaye's wife Sylvia Fine, and the respected playwright-director Abe Burrows, the show lasted only one year. This may have had something to do with Kaye's meteoric rise to movie fame following his Hollywood debut in *Up in Arms* (1944). The *Los Angeles Sentinel* (April 11, 1946) reported that both *The Danny Kaye Show*, featuring Butterfly, and *Duffy's Tavern*, featuring Eddie Green, received awards for "racial amity":

New York (Associated Press)—Duplicate awards were recently given to two outstanding radio shows for their 1945 contribution to the improvement of race relations by *Variety*, a national stage magazine. The shows honored were *Duffy's Tavern*, sponsored by Bristol-Myers on NBC, and Danny Kaye's program, a CBS Pabst sponsored show. Abe Burrows did the original script for *Duffy's Tavern*, which features a Negro waiter. No attempt was made to build laughs by making Eddie Green, who is a Negro, perpetuate the weakness(es) that have been the stock-and-trade of all Negro characterizations. "Green clicks as a waiter not because he's a Negro but because he is a good comedian," *Variety*'s citation reads. "Similarly the Goodman Ace treatment of the Butterfly McQueen role on the Kaye show offers further evidence that it isn't necessary to resort to stereotypes," *Variety* declared. "In neither case does the show ask the Negro to follow the pattern of stock characterization that belittles his people. It's proof, too, that it isn't necessary to capitalize on the weakness of any minority group to get laughs. As such, both programs may well set an example on how to combat racial intolerance and misunderstanding of minorities. Neither Butterfly McQueen nor Eddie Green sells the people short."[6]

On June 16, 1946, Butterfly joined Danny Kaye and Carmen Miranda in *Here's to the Veterans*, and on September 27, 1947, Butterfly was featured with Willie Bryant in *Harlem Hospitality*. Once again she raised laughs by sending herself up. Butterfly: "When I first sang before an audience they all clapped." Willie Bryant: "Applause, huh?" Butterfly: "Well, not exactly. They clapped their hands over their ears."[7]

In 1944 David O. Selznick called upon Butterfly to appear in *Since You Went Away*, his lavish tribute to the American family on the home front during the Second World War. In his book *David O. Selznick's Hollywood* (1980), Ronald Haver says that Selznick "had a particular fondness for the actress, whose distinctive high-pitched voice and comedic ability had been one of the enduring delights of *Gone With the Wind*."[8]

Since You Went Away ("the four most important words since *Gone With the Wind*" claimed Selznick) stars Claudette Colbert as Anne Hilton, the mother of Jane (Jennifer Jones) and "Brig" (Shirley Temple), who keep the home fires burning while their husband and father is abroad in the military. Hattie McDaniel was one member of a large supporting cast. She played Fidelia, the loyal maid and confidante to the Hilton family. However, Butterfly's small role as the leader of a group of giggling black Women's Army Corps (WAC) recruits in the famous train station sequence did not survive the final editing. At a sneak preview of the film, some real-life black WAC recruits took offence at the scene and complained. Selznick agreed to delete it, and he then replaced it with a positive image of a handsome black soldier (Bobby Johnson) saying farewell to his wife (Dorothy Dandridge) and son (Shelby Bacon) before he leaves for war. Some sources erroneously include *Since You Went Away* in Butterfly's list of film credits. In later years, in her one-woman shows, and in press interviews, Butterfly proudly boasted that, in spite of Hattie McDaniel's warning that she would not work in Hollywood again, after *Gone With the Wind*, "Mr." Selznick had put her into two more films, while he only put "Mammy" into one.

The second Selznick movie Butterfly refers to is *Duel in the Sun* (1946), for which the producer also took screenplay credit. In this grandiose and controversial saga of Texas in the 1880s, she survived the final editing as Vashti, cook, nurse, and general cleaning and serving maid of the Spanish Bit ranch where most of the action takes place. In an attempt to surpass *Gone With the Wind*, Selznick spent millions of dollars on *Duel in the Sun*. It was made in true epic style, with stunning Technicolor photography, a majestic music score by Dimitri Tiomkin, contributions by several directors (King Vidor is the only one who is credited; others, like Josef von Sternberg and William Dieterle, walked off the project), a host of stars, including Jennifer Jones, Gregory Peck, Joseph Cotten, Lionel Barrymore, Lillian Gish, and Walter Huston, and a prologue spoken by Orson Welles. The sensational (for their day) scenes of sex and violence earned the film its alternative title of *Lust in the Dust*, but the film received poor reviews. Bosley Crowther wrote in the *New York Times*: "Mr. Selznick can't long hide the fact that his multimillion-dollar western is a spectacularly disappointing job."[9]

Despite the negative reaction from the critics, *Duel in the Sun* became a gold mine—one of the biggest money-makers in cinema history—because audiences flocked to see the film that various groups condemned for its loose moral tone, disrespect for religion, and violence. However, Selznick was disappointed when his epic western failed to repeat the success of *Gone With the Wind* at the 1946 Oscars. The film received only two nominations: for Jennifer Jones (Best Actress) and Lillian Gish (Best Supporting Actress). For the third time in her career, Butterfly had the distinction of acting scenes with Best Actress and Best Supporting Actress nominees (in *Gone With the Wind* with Vivien Leigh and Hattie McDaniel and in *Mildred Pierce* with Joan Crawford and Ann Blyth).

Not everyone disliked *Duel in the Sun*. Charles Higham and Joel Greenberg in *Hollywood in the Forties* (1968) describe it as "large of gesture, florid and monumental, . . . [it has] an almost operatic quality, each bravura set-piece shot, edited and scored for maximum kinetic effect. . . . This was film-making in the grand manner, utterly self-confident and self-sufficient, its plastic splendour ultimately canceling out its colossal lack of taste."[10] In 1997, the celebrated film director Martin Scorsese recalled in *A Personal Journey with Martin Scorsese through American Movies* that he first saw *Duel in the Sun* at the age of four in 1947: "From the opening titles I was mesmerized. The bright blasts of deliriously vibrant color, the gunshots, the savage intensity of the music, the burning sun, the overt sexuality. A flawed film, maybe. Yet the hallucinatory quality of the imagery has never weakened for me over the years."[11] It has remained one of Scorsese's favorite films and has been a major influence on him.

Having won an Oscar for playing the saintly Bernadette of Lourdes in the religious drama *The Song of Bernadette* (1943), Selznick cast Jennifer Jones against type in *Duel in the Sun* as the tempestuous Pearl Chavez, "a wild-flower, sprung from the hard clay, quick to blossom and early to die."[12] Pearl's "bad" side is associated with her sexually promiscuous Native American mother, and her "good" side with her father, a white, aristocratic Southern gentleman. After their deaths, Pearl enters the lives of the McCanles family, who are also divided between the "good" and the "bad." The genteel Southern lady, Laura Belle (Lillian Gish), and her oldest son Jesse (Joseph Cotten), are good, while her husband, the Senator (Lionel Barrymore), and younger son, Lewt (Gregory Peck), are bad. Consequently, Pearl finds herself torn between the good and bad members of the family. As a woman of mixed race, Pearl fits the Hollywood stereotype of sensuality and tragedy. Her attempts to become "respectable" by posing as a Southern lady, like Laura Belle, and to marry Lewt are doomed. In fact, Pearl is not that far removed from a Hollywood stereotype of African American women: the "tragic mulatto" who is described by Donald Bogle as "likeable—even sympathetic (because of her white blood, no doubt)—and the audience believes that the girl's life could have been productive and happy had she not been a 'victim' of divided racial inheritance."[13] Perhaps the best known example of the "tragic mulatto" is Julie LaVerne in *Show Boat*, filmed in 1929, 1936, and 1951. After arriving at the Spanish Bit ranch, the cantankerous Senator racially abuses her: "How they come to name you Pearl? Couldn't have had much eye for colour . . . better to have called you Pocahontas or Minnie Ha Ha!" But she is embraced and given a warm welcome by Laura Belle, who convinces her she that she can become a lady.

When Butterfly makes her first appearance as Vashti, she is at her most wistful and endearing. Bustling into Laura Belle's room with some "medicine" (brandy), her earrings dangling away and dazzling in the light, she asks if she can get married, completely oblivious to the fact that she is living on a ranch in the middle of nowhere. Laura Belle humors her, but not in a condescending or patronizing way. She does it gently, asking the servant girl whom she would like to marry. Vashti responds: "Oh, nobody in particular, ma'am. I just thought I'd kinda like to get married." Not wishing to offend Vashti, Laura Belle tells her she may marry whenever she wishes, and that she'll think about a possible husband. After Vashti leaves the room, Laura Belle informs Pearl: "I'm afraid I'll never be able to train her properly. And as to marriage!" However, Vashti departs from the stereotypical comic Hollywood maid for she has something in common with Laura Belle: they are both living in a dream world.

Laura Belle has tried to recreate a little bit of the Deep South in her remote, dusty, desolate Texas home. Importing and employing a black servant girl to wait on her family is part of this. But Spanish Bit isn't a Southern plantation, and Vashti is not like the servants Laura Belle would have had back home. She is dizzy and dreamy, and shares the sweet, gentle nature of

Laura Belle. She bears no resemblance to the Vashti of Niven Busch's 1941 novel, in which she is old and cunning in her dealing with white people, and married to another servant, Old Eli, a former slave.[14]

After Laura Belle plays "Beautiful Dreamer" on the piano, it becomes her theme tune, and this can be heard almost every time she appears in the film. This is what Laura Belle and Vashti are: beautiful dreamers, and Selznick ensures Butterfly's physical appearance conforms to this. He pays careful attention to how Vashti looks. Gone are the scruffy, torn clothes and head rags she wore as Prissy throughout *Gone With the Wind*. Vashti's clothes are much smarter and stylized. In the seven scenes she has in *Duel in the Sun*, she wears something different, and each costume and colourful bandanna have been beautifully and carefully designed, and they suit the mood of each scene in which she appears.

In her second scene, taking an inventory of the food store with Pearl, Vashti wistfully croons the Negro spiritual "Sometimes I Feel Like a Motherless Child." When Pearl asks her to make the list, Vashti reveals that she cannot write and that "Mr. Lewt once called me an empty head." One can only feel sympathy for this mysterious young black woman who is illiterate and feels like a "motherless child." In another scene, at nighttime, when Laura Belle sends Vashti to fetch Pearl to meet Mr. Jubal Crabbe (Walter Huston), the "Sin Killer," the servant girl is completely in a world of her own. In Pearl's room, Vashti plays with some beads and takes her time passing on the message. When Pearl asked her why she is so slow, Vashti replies: "I don't rightly know, Miss Pearl, except I always have so much to remember." At the barbecue, an excited Vashti says to herself, "When I'm married I'm gonna have lots and lots of parties. But who'll do all the work when I gives my party?" The next shot is revealing. A black boy and a white boy are seen observing the party from the branch of a tree. So Vashti is *not* the only black person on the Spanish Bit ranch or the surrounding neighborhood, and yet we never see her in the company of other black people, or making contact with the boy in the tree. In her final scene, after Laura Belle has died, a tearful Vashti tells Jesse: "Miss McCanles she treated Miss Pearl awfully good. She treated everybody awful good. Even me." In *Duel in the Sun*, none of the characters are nasty to Vashti, not even the evil Lewt. Perhaps Selznick wanted Vashti to be a more sympathetic character than Prissy. There is no Scarlett to slap her in this film.

Selznick's attention to detail—and his extravagance—was mentioned by the columnist Ruth Waterbury in *Photoplay* magazine in May 1947: "The scene where Butterfly McQueen enters Jennifer Jones's room at night only takes a second, but because Selznick wanted the kerosene lamp to light the darkness of Butterfly's piquant little face in one particular glowing way, it took an hour to get it. That means a single second cost $6,500, which was the production cost per hour. You can multiply these details by a hundred to understand the staggering cost of the present picture."[15]

In addition to film critics, the National Association for the Advancement of Colored People (NAACP) was unhappy with *Duel in the Sun*: "Selznick was not an NAACP favorite. . . . when the movie was released, Roy Wilkins of the NAACP called it 'colossal trash.' Members objected to the role played by Butterfly McQueen and to the stereotyped portrayals of Native Americans."[16]

It is possible that the NAACP protests had a direct impact on Butterfly. Following her appearance in *Duel in the Sun*, the actress issued a statement in which she said she would no longer play stupid maids. It was a brave stand against Hollywood stereotyping. Before Butterfly made her stand, others who had made protests included Fredi Washington, Lena Horne, and Paul Robeson. Gary Null says in *Black Hollywood: The Negro in Motion Pictures* (1975): "[Butterfly] said that she would never again play a scatterbrained maid or a superstitious comic servant. Like Fredi Washington before her, she left her film career behind. She had played her particular stereotype too well, and producers were not prepared to offer her anything else. True to her word, she never appeared in her old image again."[17]

In the 1930s Fredi Washington rose to fame after playing the light-skinned Peola, who passes for white, in the melodrama *Imitation of Life* (1934), but her steadfast refusal to play maids in the movies brought an abrupt end to her Hollywood career. In 1942, when Lena Horne became the first African American star to negotiate a seven-year studio contract (with MGM), she had to attend a meeting with the studio head, Louis B. Mayer, and the producer Arthur Freed. She asked her father, Teddy Horne, to accompany her, and he made it clear that his daughter was not going to play anyone's maid. Says Lena's daughter, Gail Lumet Buckley:

> Teddy Horne cast a suspicious eye on the whole situation. . . . He suddenly saw his lamb among the Hollywood wolves, and he flew out to California for Lena's next Freed-Mayer meeting. The studio executives were no doubt as impressed with Teddy's studied coolness as they were with his Sulka tie and handmade shoes. "Mr. Mayer," said Teddy, "I have very few illusions about the movie business." He studied his perfectly manicured nails. "The only Negroes I ever see are menials, or Tarzan extras. I don't see what the movies have to offer my daughter. I can hire a maid for her; why should she act one?" L. B. was both sincere and conciliatory. "Mr. Horne, I can assure you that we would never allow anything to embarrass either you or your daughter."[18]

Lena Horne signed the contract and did not play a maid, but in the same year that she signed with MGM, Paul Robeson turned his back on Hollywood after publicly denouncing his latest Hollywood movie, Twentieth Century Fox's *Tales of Manhattan*. He had tried to bring dignity and humanity to the role of a poor Southern sharecropper, but after the film's release in September 1942, he came under fire for perpetuating a racial stereotype. He agreed with his critics and publicly stated in *PM* (September 22, 1942) that he "wouldn't blame any Negro for picketing the film. . . . when I first read the script I told them it was silly," but he had hoped he could change it during the filming. Two days later, he was quoted in the *New York Times* (September 24, 1942): "It turned out to be the same old thing—the Negro solving his problem by singing his way to glory. This is very offensive to my people. It makes the Negro child-like and innocent and is in the old plantation tradition. But Hollywood says you can't make the Negro in any other role because it won't be box office in the South. The South wants its Negroes in the old style." The film historian Thomas Cripps describes the dilemma Robeson faced in Hollywood in 1942: "Robeson, despondent and bitter, told an interviewer that his film career was at an end. . . . Forced to choose between long-standing loyalty to cinema and his faith in the politics of the left, he chose the latter and blasted the picture he had liked enough to appear in and fight to change."[19]

In Britain, in 1948, Peter Noble praised Butterfly for making a stand against Hollywood stereotyping in *The Negro in Films*, his pioneering book about black actors in popular cinema. Regrettably, few books about African Americans in films published since that time have bothered to acknowledge Butterfly's sacrifice. Noble says:

Undoubtedly she has since found herself in the cleft stick which awaits all independent Negro players—to act stereotypes or starve. Nevertheless it is to be hoped that her courageous stand will have some effect on Hollywood opinion, and in encouraging Negro rebels. And in any case, one must applaud her strength of character in taking such a decision for her principles at a time when her acting in *Mildred Pierce* has served to indicate her talent for comedy and her perfect film timing (and, incidentally, resulted in her being offered several comic maid roles—which she refused). . . . Butterfly McQueen is on the fringe of a promising film career. Hollywood producers have said that although she is such a notable comedienne she has the capabilities of playing strong dramatic roles, but as to that events will give a further indication. At any rate this actress has a flair for cinema and a love of acting. It would be heartening to be able to record incidents of other Negro players making protests against Hollywood's ever-prevalent colour prejudice, but unfortunately this has not happened often.[20]

Notes

1. *Jubilee* program review in *California Eagle*, July 13, 1944, reprinted in Henry T. Sampson, *Swingin' on the Ether Waves: A Chronological History of African Americans in Radio and Television Broadcasting, 1925–1955* (Lanham, Md., and Oxford: Scarecrow Press, 2005), 1:511–12.

2. AFRS, *Jubilee*, c. August 1943.

3. AFRS, *Jubilee*, June 26, 1944.

4. Butterfly McQueen, *Miscellanea 4* (see appendix C).

5. "Butterfly McQueen Shines on the Dinah Shore Program" (review), *Chicago Defender*, December 2, 1944, reprinted in Sampson, *Swingin' on the Ether Waves*, 1:524.

6. "Two Radio Shows Receive Awards for Racial Amity," *Los Angeles Sentinel*, April 11, 1946, reprinted in Sampson, *Swingin' on the Ether Waves*, 1:591.

7. *Harlem Hospitality*, September 27, 1947, quoted in Sampson, *Swingin' on the Ether Waves*, 1:660.

8. Ronald Haver, *David O. Selznick's Hollywood* (New York: Bonanza Books, 1980), 362.

9. Bosley Crowther, *The New York Times*, May 8, 1947, quoted in W. Franklyn Moshier, *The Films of Jennifer Jones* (San Francisco: W. Franklyn Moshier, 1978), 68.

10. Charles Higham and Joel Greenberg, *Hollywood in the Forties* (London: A. Zwemmer, 1968), 133.

11. Martin Scorsese and Michael Henry Wilson, *A Personal Journey with Martin Scorsese through American Movies* (London: Faber and Faber, 1997), 31.

12. David O. Selznick's prologue to *Duel in the Sun*, spoken by Orson Welles and quoted in Moshier, *Films of Jennifer Jones*, 65.

13. Donald Bogle, *Toms, Coons, Mulattoes, Mammies and Bucks: An Interpretive History of Blacks in American Films* (New York: Bantam Books, 1974), 9.

14. Niven Busch, *Duel in the Sun* (1941; London: W. H. Allen, 1947), 26.

15. Ruth Waterbury in *Photoplay*, May 1947.

16. Patrick McGee, *From Shane to Kill Bill: Rethinking the Western* (Malden, Mass., and Oxford: Blackwell, 2007), 65.

17. Gary Null, *Black Hollywood: The Negro in Motion Pictures* (Secaucus, N.J.: Citadel Press, 1975), 109.

18. Gail Lumet Buckley, *The Hornes: An American Family* (London: Weidenfeld and Nicholson, 1987), 156.

19. Thomas Cripps, *Slow Fade to Black: The Negro in American Film, 1900–1942* (London, Oxford, and New York: Oxford University Press, 1977), 384.

20. Peter Noble, *The Negro in Films* (London: Skelton Robinson, 1948), 166, 169.

CHAPTER NINE

~

What Ever Happened to Butterfly McQueen?

I keep myself low profile because you're glad to see me when I do come back.

—Butterfly McQueen during a performance of her nightclub act at the famous Reno Sweeney club in New York in 1978

After Butterfly turned her back on Hollywood, she found herself almost unemployable in show business. In spite of being closely identified with the role of Prissy, and unable to shake off the stereotypical image of the simple-minded maid, she valiantly pursued her acting career. Mostly she earned a living by taking any job that came her way. "Any honest job I have taken," she told Sarah Gristwood in an interview in *The Guardian*.[1] At various times in the 1950s and 1960s Butterfly folded underwear in a factory, dispatched taxicabs in the Bronx section of New York, operated a restaurant, sold toys at Macy's department store in New York City, and managed a theatre group for New York's YMCA. She also worked as a cinema usher in Augusta, Georgia, a real-life maid to a wealthy couple in Atlanta, a seamstress at Saks Fifth Avenue department store, and a paid companion to an elderly lady on Long Island. An off-stage role she thoroughly enjoyed was that of Santa Claus at children's hospitals. She said that children were delighted with a black female Santa with a high voice. All these jobs were a far cry from the sound stages of the Hollywood studios where she had pursued a career in films. Undoubtedly she would have returned to the film capital if the right part had been offered. Butterfly waited and waited, but no offers came. Hollywood was not interested in employing an African American actress who had defiantly made a stand against racial stereotyping.

Shortly after quitting Hollywood, Butterfly surfaced in one more film, and it would be her last for over twenty years. However, *Killer Diller* (1948) was not seen very widely. Produced independently, outside Hollywood, for black audiences, this low-budget comedy had a prologue featuring Butterfly as a secretary who chases after the comedian Dusty Fletcher, famous for his catchphrase "Open the door, Richard!" It was followed by a "live" stage revue, performed in front of a black audience. There was hardly any plot to this film, but audiences at the time would have enjoyed the guest appearances of such artistes as the King Cole Trio (featuring a young Nat "King" Cole) and the show-stopping Clark Brothers, who gave a dazzling tap dancing routine that rivaled the Nicholas Brothers.

Today, *Killer Diller* is best known for an early film appearance by one of black America's comedy favorites, the quick-witted and sharp-tongued stand-up comedienne Jackie "Moms" Mabley. Two years earlier she had appeared in *Big Timers* with Stepin Fetchit, directed by Josh Binney, who also directed her in *Killer Diller*. Mel Watkins observes that *Killer Diller* was "even less restricted by plot or storyline" than Binney's earlier film, stringing together a succession of musical and comedy routines on a thin plot involving a magician whose disappearing act goes haywire and disrupts performances at an all-black theatre. Watkins continues,

> The skeletal plot allowed Binney to shoot most of the film in a theatre before a black audience. Dusty Fletcher stars as the inept magician and is supported by a cast that includes Moms Mabley, Butterfly McQueen, George Wiltshire (longtime straight man for Fletcher and Pigmeat Markham), Nat "King" Cole, and Andy Kirk and his orchestra. Fletcher is rambunctious and mildly suggestive as he performs a few set pieces with McQueen, but Moms Mabley is curiously disengaged here, uncharacteristically having to prod the live audience for laughter. Although its inane, Keystone Kops–inspired chase scenes are distracting, the movie manages to capture some of the tenor of a live stage show.[2]

In 1949 Butterfly set out on a tour of vaudeville theaters on the East Coast of America. She chatted about her film work and sang a number of songs including an old British music hall favorite that she kept in her repertoire for four decades, "I Never Cried So Much in All My Life," popularized by Gracie Fields. On January 16, 1950, Butterfly made her television debut in *Give Us Our Dream*, an edition of CBS's dramatic anthology series *Studio One*. Josephine Hull, who went on to win that year's Oscar for Best Supporting Actress for *Harvey*, was also in the cast. Later that year Butterfly was reunited with *Cabin in the Sky*'s Ethel Waters in a popular television series,

Beulah. Filmed in the Bronx section of New York and debuting on October 3, 1950, ABC's *Beulah* was the first nationally broadcast weekly television series starring an African American. This half-hour situation comedy revolved around the whimsical antics of a conscientious, lovable, middle-aged black domestic called Beulah, and the Hendersons, the white family who employed her. Ethel Waters played Beulah, and Butterfly her feather-brained sidekick, Oriole, during the series first two seasons from 1950 to 1952. In April 1952 there was a major cast change when the Hollywood veteran Hattie McDaniel was scheduled to replace Ethel. Ill health prevented Hattie from appearing as Beulah, and the part went to Louise Beavers until she decided to leave the role in September 1953.

Oriole is Beulah's best friend, a scatterbrained maid who works for the family next door and spends time with Beulah in the Hendersons' kitchen. In addition to generating laughs with her silly behavior, Oriole is always on the lookout for a husband. The dialogue Butterfly and Ethel were expected to utter is not far removed from the self-deprecating lines Butterfly had sometimes spoken in movies and in radio shows like *Jubilee* (see chapter 8). For instance, in an episode from 1950, Oriole enters the Hendersons' kitchen and finds Beulah knitting. "What are you doing? Knitting?" she asks. Replies Beulah, sarcastically: "I'm not baking a cake." Oriole: "I wish you'd teach me to knit sometime." Beulah: "Maybe I'll take a year off one day and try!"[3] The actor Percy "Bud" Harris, who was cast as Bill, Beulah's long-suffering but shiftless boyfriend, quit the series early on. He complained that the show's writers were forcing him to portray Bill as a racist caricature, an "Uncle Tom," and participate in comedy scenes he found degrading to black people. Dooley Wilson, who had played Sam in the wartime movie classic *Casablanca*, took over the role of Bill.

Undoubtedly Butterfly must have sympathized with Harris, but this was one of her highest-paid jobs, earning her $400 a week, and she hadn't worked much as an actress since quitting Hollywood in 1946. To her credit, in some of her scenes, Butterfly shines as a comedy actress *par excellence*, generating laughs with her dizzy antics that are both amusing and appealing, but too often, the self-deprecating humor jars, and has racist overtones.

Butterfly did not have happy memories of working with Ethel. In later interviews, she expressed the difficulties she faced with the tough star of *Beulah*: "She wasn't pleasant. I went on and sure enough, she would call me 'manure.' She'd been to the University of Hard Knocks, and so she used four-letter words. And she used another four-letter word. A bedroom word. And I was so embarrassed because there was a little girl there. And do you know who that little girl was? Leslie Uggams."[4] Uggams went on to become a popular television personality, as both a singer and an actress. She is best known for her role as Kizzy in *Roots* (1977). Butterfly claimed that Ethel became jealous because she was getting all the laughs: "She was the star, and as such she used her power. The backstage atmosphere became very tense. I decided to give up the part."[5]

When Butterfly left the cast, Ruby Dandridge, the mother of Dorothy, took over the role of Oriole for the final season. After *Beulah* ended in September 1953, there would be no regular series starring a black actress again for fifteen years when Diahann Carroll took the leading role in the popular comedy series *Julia*.

Beulah was popular with viewers, but it came under fire from critics for perpetuating racial stereotypes. Ethel was singled out for betraying her other outstanding accomplishments on stage and in films. At its annual convention in June 1951, the National Association for the Advancement of Colored People (NAACP) condemned *Beulah* and another popular sitcom, *Amos 'n' Andy*. Fifty years later, in 2001, Donald Bogle summarized:

> ABC's decision to cast Ethel Waters proved a wise one. Improbable as it may seem, she truly lent the series some distinction and a lopsided credibility. Her presence also indicated—early on—that viewers might overlook weak story lines or poorly developed characters if they liked the people on-screen. Waters endowed the show with a subtext that made *Beulah* far more than it appeared on the surface. . . . Occupying a unique place in the national consciousness, Ethel Waters was perceived as a woman of emotional depth and resilience; a woman whose spirit and drive had enabled her to endure in a sometimes tough and cruel world. . . . As played by Waters, Beulah is hard not to like. Gracing this nothing character with her own profound warmth and tenderness as well as a modicum of conviction, Waters transformed Beulah into a knowing earth mother, able to unravel life's tangled (albeit trivial) difficulties and to make everything right.[6]

In spite of the success of *Beulah*, there were few openings in television for Butterfly. On June 11, 1951, in *Lux Video Theatre*, another dramatic anthology series for CBS, she appeared with Lynn Bari in *Weather for Today*. A few years later, on March 23, 1957, she was seen in NBC's celebrated *Hallmark Hall of Fame* production of Marc Connelly's *The Green Pastures*. This classic American drama, which reenacted scenes from the Bible using black actors, was first staged on Broadway in 1930 and was filmed in Hollywood in 1936 by Warner Brothers. For the television version, opera singer William Warfield was cast in the lead as "De Lawd." The production was nominated for three Emmys (American television's equivalent of the Oscar): Best Single

Program of the Year; Best Direction (George Schaefer); and Best Teleplay Writing (Marc Connelly). For years, stage and television revivals of *The Green Pastures* provided work for black actors, but not all of them were happy with the play. Though Ossie Davis accepted the role of Gabriel in the 1951 Broadway revival, he later said: "It was a classic example of the kind of plays about black people that I was in a great hurry to get away from. I objected to its patronizing view of black religion. In *Green Pastures*, the people are simple and childlike, walking around heaven all day, having a singing good time. Their constant life of devotion was focused on De Lawd, a benign father figure who addressed them, one and all, as children. Heaven in their view was one vast fish-fry celebration, presided over by De Lawd."[7]

In 1951 Butterfly's dream of staging a one-woman show at Carnegie Recital Hall in New York City was finally realized. She invested her life savings of $15,000 into this production, which extended her vaudeville act, with some dancing and dramatic recitations. A limited engagement (just three performances from October 14 to 16), it was considered a limited artistic success but proved to be a financial disaster for the actress because so few were interested in seeing her. Butterfly lost her life savings.

Butterfly never gave up hope of a career on the stage. In late 1951 and early 1952, she was a member of the Negro Drama Guild's touring production of Mary Chase's comedy-drama *Harvey*, with an all-black cast that featured Dooley Wilson as Elwood P. Dowd. He's a mild-mannered, pleasant man, who just happens (he says) to have an invisible friend resembling a six-foot rabbit. This was the role made famous by Hollywood star James Stewart, who had just received an Oscar nomination for his memorable performance in the 1950 film version. Butterfly was cast as Myrtle Mae Simmons. Also in the cast was Lorenzo Tucker, who was once known as "The Black Valentino" for his appearances in films made for black audiences in the 1920s and 1930s. He later recalled: "We were putting on *Harvey* for black audiences at town halls and black colleges, and we had to drive all the way there in two station wagons from New York."[8]

In 1953 Butterfly was "featured" in Lawrence Langner's *Once Married, Twice Shy* at the Westport Country Playhouse in Westport, Connecticut. Elaine Stritch starred in this comedy that opened on July 27 and closed on August 1, canceling plans to move to New York. On July 31, 1956, she opened in an intriguing off-Broadway musical called *The World's My Oyster* at the Actor's Playhouse. Its coauthor, the African American Lorenzo Fuller, also had a starring role and worked as the show's musical director. In 1948 Fuller had introduced "Too Darn Hot" in Cole Porter's Broadway smash *Kiss Me, Kate*. The plot concerned two New Yorkers who go searching for pearls on a long-forgotten South Sea Island. Butterfly played the island's leader, with a name almost as fantastic as her own: Queen Elizabeth Victoria, but the show lasted only a month, closing on September 2. One of the choreographers was Louis Johnson, who later won a Tony award for his work on *Purlie* (1970).

First screened in 1956, Mike Wallace's late-night television show *Night Beat* was the vehicle that brought Wallace to prominence as one of America's most enduring and popular television personalities. *Night Beat* was transmitted live from a studio in New York, and in the early part of 1957 Butterfly made a guest appearance. In a revealing interview she explained that she became an actress because it was a hobby when she was a nurse in training school. After failing chemistry, staff at the nursing school told her "you'll make a good actress" and advised her to change careers. She told Wallace: "I had never studied to become an actress, and I didn't understand much about the theatre at the time that I came into it." When questioned about how Hattie McDaniel felt playing Mammy in *Gone With the Wind*, Butterfly explained: "She was in seventh heaven because she had had ups and downs in vaudeville and to get to Hollywood, that was just heaven for her." Wallace then asked her about the problems black actors faced on the set of *Gone With the Wind*. Butterfly revealed that she demanded to be taken to the location in a long limousine, not a "cramped little car," adding, "it wasn't Mr. Selznick's fault that we were packed in this old car while the other white actresses had a limousine. In every production there's always somebody that's frustrated and they take it out by doing something unkind to the negro, and this happens nearly everywhere you go." Wallace pushed further: "I gather that what you objected to was that negroes were treated as second-class citizens by Hollywood back then. Do you feel that it has changed?" Butterfly replied: "Of course it has changed. In my very next picture with Mr. Selznick, *Since You Went Away*, I rode out in a long limousine all by myself (laughs)." Reacting to another question about the treatment of black people in America, Butterfly replied: "I wouldn't for a million dollars sit here and try to say what the negro as a whole is. We are human beings that less than a hundred years ago were in slavery. We had no education. We had no funds. We had no people to whom we could turn to help us. We were brought over here to work the fields. We nearly all have a common beginning, but I'm only speaking for my family. I think we were brought over here as slaves and I think it's marvelous that less than a hundred years now, ninety-one years to be exact, I have a fair measure of independence. I owe this to my thrifty grandmother and my mother that I am now the third generation of property owners in America." Wallace asked Butterfly how she earned her living when not acting. She replied: "I earn my living the same way my ancestors did. I am a worker. If I can't find the right role I want to do, or the right people I want to work with in the theatre, I do other things. I've worked in the factories. I've worked as a salesgirl. I'm carrying on the tradition of my family. I've been a worker, I wasn't born in the theatre. My daddy was a stevedore, my mother was a domestic. One grandfather ran a woodyard. He was an independent businessman. The wealthiest member of our family was Bill Nabey of Augusta, Georgia who was a butcher for Mr. Miles on Milton Road. My next job will be what I did for Macy's last Christmas, I'll be selling toys. I start that on April 13. Now that's my job for the spring. In the fall the Negro Drama Players have asked me to be their leading lady for *Bell, Book and Candle* and *Springtime for Henry*. We're touring and if any clubs, colleges or any ladies garden clubs want us to appear, please contact Mr. Michael Padoli, 171 West 75th Street, Trafalgar 71001." Wallace closed the interview with the following testament: "Butterfly McQueen, occasional star of television and films, is distinctly like no one else in both public and private life. To each she brings simplicity and honesty expressed, I think you'll agree, in a voice that rather defies description."

A few years after their appearance in *Harvey*, Butterfly and Lorenzo Tucker were reunited for the Negro Drama Players' production of John Van Druten's comedy *Bell, Book and Candle*, mentioned by Butterfly in the Wallace interview. This toured the Southern United States, much the same way that the tour of *Harvey* did five years earlier. Tucker later recalled that part of the funding for the production was raised by Butterfly.[9] Sometime in the late 1950s Butterfly was featured in an adaptation of Molière's classic stage comedy *School for Wives* at the Theatre Marquee. No further details have come to light.

Following her mother's death in 1957, Butterfly spent some time in Augusta, Georgia, where her mother had lived. She took a course in nursing at the Georgia Medical School and managed Belles Noires Enfante, a community service club for black children. To support the project she sold peanut butter sandwiches and cold drinks in a small shop. She gave music lessons and also appeared in her own local radio show. During that time, William Hughes was growing up in Augusta. He moved away in 1964 and, despite countless visits, never lived in the South again. He became a professional management consultant and trainer as well as an author of fiction and nonfiction. His memories of Augusta in the 1950s led to the publication of *Snapshots of a Faded Past*. In this book, he recalled the time Butterfly worked at his local cinema:

At one point, the Lennox went classy and hired an usher, in fact she was a celebrity usher. Butterfly McQueen, long past the prime of her career, which peaked with her role in *Gone With the Wind*, decided, for some reason, to settle in Augusta. She was hired by the Lennox to be an usher. She wore a uniform, like the ushers in the large movie houses in New York, and took her duties quite seriously. She sternly faced down the kids, ordering them to discard their chewing gum, because they would throw it on the floor or stick it on the backs of the seats. She kept a broom and dustbin handy to sweep every bit of paper or other trash that was visible on the floor. She gave the Lennox a quality and class that it had never had before. Ironically, she was working at the theater when the Lennox showed *Duel in the Sun*, in which Butterfly played a mirror role to *Gone With the Wind*, a high-pitched voice house servant. One wonders what she thought as she watched her image on the screen and heard the laughter of the kids in the theater.

Butterfly McQueen remained in Augusta, doing various things and living in various places. At one point she lived directly across from our house, in a little apartment. Long after she had left the Lennox Theater and moved from the little apartment across from our house, we had forgotten she was still in Augusta. . . . The world knew Butterfly McQueen, but, ironically, most of the people of Augusta knew her the least.[10]

At various times between May 1963 and July 1965 Butterfly worked as one of the tour guides on weekends at the Stone Mountain Park, near Atlanta, Georgia. This restored plantation had been transformed into a museum of Confederate times. Butterfly's tasks included greeting visitors, signing autographs, and posing for photographs. The job ended unhappily for Butterfly when she complained about the unauthorized use of her name and photograph. She sued her employers for $100,000 in damages but lost the case. Afterwards, she was unemployed for a long period. On January 10, 1966, the *New York Times* reported that she had appealed to a Georgia congressman for help in getting a job. "Miss McQueen, now 55 years old and a resident of Augusta, said she had not worked in more than six months and that the money she made in the role of Scarlett O'Hara's maid was gone long ago. The Atlanta Constitution's Washington Bureau said today that Miss McQueen telephoned Representative Charles L. Walter of Atlanta for aid. 'I would like theater work if I could get it, or I could do some reception or singing,' she said."[11] A year later she moved to Harlem and plunged herself into antipoverty work, and took a job at a soul food restaurant. She defined herself at the time through her commitment to the "black family." In spite of her hardship, in 1967 Butterfly reportedly declined MGM's offer to make personal appearances at screenings of their reissue of *Gone With the Wind* in return for expenses.

Meanwhile, theatre work continued to elude her. In 1959 she unsuccessfully auditioned for a role in the Broadway musical *Destry*, and in the late

Butterfly in *Gone With the Wind* (1939). *Courtesy of Turner Entertainment Co.*

Vivien Leigh and Butterfly in *Gone With the Wind. Courtesy of Turner Entertainment Co.*

Hattie McDaniel, Olivia de Havilland, and Vivien Leigh in *Gone With the Wind*.
Courtesy of Turner Entertainment Co.

Butterfly. *Courtesy of the author*

A portrait of Butterfly by Albert Leonard. *Courtesy of Albert Leonard*

Butterfly and Eleanor Powell in *I Dood It* (1943). *Courtesy of Turner Entertainment Co.*

Butterfly (1969). *Courtesy of the author*

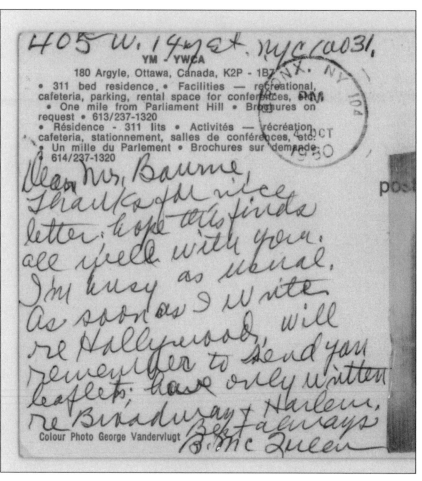

Butterfly's postcard message to Stephen Bourne (1980). *Courtesy of the author*

Raising a flutter at Reno's

SQUEAKY-VOICED Butterfly McQueen, best remembered for one movie ("Gone With the Wind") and one line in it ("I don't know nothin' about birthin' babies, Miz Scarlett") makes her cafe debut Sunday and Monday at Reno Sweeney, 126 W. 13th St. The act will include a question and answer session about her days in Hollywood. Show times are at 9 and 11 p.m.
— MARTIN BURDEN.

Butterfly at Reno Sweeney (1978). *Courtesy of the author*

Butterfly (1989). *Photo by Geraint Lewis © Geraint Lewis*

1960s, she also lost out on a role in the black-cast Broadway production of *Hello, Dolly!* It was alleged that the star of the show, Pearl Bailey, didn't want her. Butterfly's stage career looked up in 1964 when she won a role in *The Athenian Touch*, an off-Broadway musical with music by Willard Straight and lyrics by David Eddy. Set in Athens in the third year of the Eighty-eighth Olympiad, around 425 BC, Butterfly was cast as Ora, the servant of Attalea, a glamorous courtesan, played by Marion Marlowe. Opening at the Jan Hus Playhouse on January 14, 1964, the show included two solo numbers by Butterfly, "No Garlic Tonight" and "Look Away," but it was her show-stopping duet with Marlowe, "A Lady of Leisure," that was the big hit of the evening. *The Athenian Touch* had excellent reviews ("Bright and airy," said the *New York Times*[12]), and Butterfly was singled out by some critics: "as chirpy-voiced and as full of the Old Nick as ever" (*The New Yorker*)[13] and "that imp, is delightful . . . her renditions are pure charm" (*N. Y. World-Telegram*).[14] Was this the breakthrough she had been waiting for? It should have been. However, the show closed after just one performance. According to the sleeve notes in the 1994 CD reissue of the original cast recording: "*The Athenian Touch* joined that ever growing bank of productions which were cut short by lack of funds, poor critical notices or some other equally terminal condition. . . . After the closing, there remained sufficient funds to record the production." Thank goodness there were "sufficient funds" to record the songs, for Butterfly's numbers, especially her duet, are delightful. *The Athenian Touch* was one of the high spots of her career.

Sometime in the 1960s Butterfly was associated with the Caffe Cino, a small coffeehouse that had been opened by Joseph Cino in 1958 on Cornelia Street in New York's Greenwich Village. Though it closed ten years later, Caffe Cino became one of the most important café-theatres of the period. In fact it was instrumental in launching and popularizing the Off-Off-Broadway theatre movement. Says Wendell C. Stone: "Exactly when entertainment became a regular feature at the Caffe is uncertain, but different kinds of entertainment probably were offered almost from the beginning. Very early in the Cino's history a fortune-teller moved from table to table, reading tarot cards. At some point Taylor Mead, the 'Homosexual Clown' and star of various Warhol and other underground films, read poetry there, as did Butterfly McQueen."[15]

In 1968 Butterfly attracted some media attention—including an appearance on television in the *Mike Douglas Show*—when she joined the cast of another off-Broadway musical, *Curley McDimple*. This spoof of Shirley Temple's optimistic film character, set in Sarah's run-down theatrical boardinghouse in 1930s Manhattan, opened at the Bert Wheeler Theatre in New

York on November 22, 1967. With music and lyrics by Robert Dahdah, the story revolves around eight-year-old Curley (the Shirley Temple character), who arrives one day at the boardinghouse, looking for parents to adopt her. When Sarah's boardinghouse is threatened with closure, Curley and the boarders raise funds by putting on a vaudeville show. The original cast included Bayn Johnson as Curley and a young Bernadette Peters as Alice, one of the boarders. After Peters left the cast to star on Broadway in *George M!*, Butterfly joined the cast of *Curley McDimple* on May 9, 1968, in a role created specially for her. It was Hattie, the boardinghouse cook. Says Guy Flatley in the *New York Times*: "Miss McQueen more than justifies the star billing the producers have given her. She sings a bit, shuffles a bit, and, finally, faints a bit. In short she does the Prissy bit. And she does it with apologies to no one."[16] The role of Hattie was eliminated when she left the cast. *Curley McDimple* was a hit, running for a grand total of 991 performances, and it helped to rejuvenate Butterfly's theatrical career. Jane Stuart, who was in the cast of *Curley McDimple* at the same time as Butterfly, recalls:

> I was very young, about 19 years old, when I worked with Butterfly McQueen and I was a little shy and maybe too self centered, not as outgoing and interested in others as I am now. If I had been less shy, I would have at least attempted to spend more time and have more conversation with her. She was approachable and always sweet, but not at all outspoken. Not with us, anyway. *Curley McDimple* was a cute play. Not particularly well written, but lots of fun. Big song and tap dance numbers. Very good old timey songs. Clever. The show was a takeoff of the Shirley Temple films and all the parts were stereotypes of the characters in those films. I played the part of the mean spinster that tries to take the child away to the orphanage, there was a fabulous dancer who played the part of Bill Robinson and Butterfly played the housemaid/caretaker of the rooming house that the young leading woman and man live in. They find Curley sitting on their doorstep one day. Orphaned. Butterfly is the nurturer and confidante of Curley, not quite a Mammy, but close. Truly a stereotype. Thank goodness, her character was not a scatter brain as in *Gone With the Wind*. She was wonderful in that film, no doubt, just glad that she had a little more room in this play.
>
> Butterfly's entrance came about half an hour or more into the first act and, when she walked onto the stage, the audience went wild with cheers and applause . . . every time! And we all (the cast) felt so proud. Everybody loved her. And she delivered. The part wasn't much to work with, but she gave it her honest best. Off stage, she was very quiet. Not one to be too social with any of us. Not anti-social, but in retrospect I wonder if she didn't feel a little guarded. Not sure. We did have some real deal Southerners in the cast. Never heard anything that was unfriendly in any way. Just wonder if it had some silent effect. She did

once ask to borrow my mascara and I gladly lent it to her. She was concerned that I might not want it back, because *she* had used it. If she could only have known that I felt honored that she used it! There was one performance where we couldn't find her. Her cue came up and no one could find her. We were all worried sick, not to mention that although we improvised to keep the show moving, it made no sense to the storyline of the play. She did finally show up, backstage. The show was still on and I asked her, "Where were you? Everything okay? We were worried to death!" She whispered to me, "I was hungry and ran out to get a sandwich!" I loved her then and I love her now. She was very, very sweet.[17]

During the run of *Curley McDimple*, Butterfly met the entertainment writer Mal Vincent who, after she died, published the following tribute in *The Virginian-Pilot* (December 31, 1995):

I first met her backstage at an Off-Broadway theater when she was doing a little comedy called *Curley McDimple*. She asked if I would walk her down 41st Street to catch her bus. "I'm scared to walk down that street by myself," she said. "People are so mean now. I don't know why. They didn't used to be." She asked if I would mind if she stopped to get an ice cream cone. As we walked, she talked about *Gone With the Wind*. "Mr. Clark (Gable) was so tall and so nice—a gentleman. He made soooooooooo much money, but I didn't make much." Asked about Vivien Leigh, she admitted, "there was a lot of gossip written about Miss Vivien Leigh being mean on the set—especially to me, because, you know, she had to slap me—hard—but I knew she was acting. You know, Prissy was worrisome. I think, actually, Prissy should have been slapped." Finishing her ice cream cone, she retrieved the basket I had been carrying for her and boarded the bus to Harlem. There she lived in a one-room apartment with a cat named Mozart. Through the years, I kept in contact. She never changed, even as she aged. "No sir, I never get tired of Prissy," she said. "I make my living from her, you know. The fans are just everywhere!" In Harlem, her daily routine involved neighborhood clean-up. "Whenever I see a weed, I pull it up, and I teach the children to help," she said. She played the piano, "mostly things by Mr. Mozart." Her philosophy on racial issues was direct: "Black people have made great progress and we shouldn't take that for granted, but all black Americans should let the world know that we don't have a lot of hateful white people in this country. We need to speak up for our country. We have fine white people here and we have fine black people and we're working together. We wouldn't have gotten this far if we hadn't."[18]

On August 12, 2006, "nneprevilo" posted the following anecdote on the Internet Movie Database entitled "The Night I Met Butterfly McQueen." He recalls a brief encounter with the actress, shortly after she left the cast of *Curley McDimple*:

I was appearing off-Broadway in a play called *Le Beste* back in the '70s. One night after the show, I stopped by an ice cream parlor on 72nd and Amsterdam Avenue, on the way home. While standing there trying to decide, I noticed the people to the right of me looking in my direction and whispering. When I took notice of who they were talking about, I looked to my left and there stood Butterfly McQueen, looking up at the menu! I was in shock, so I leaned down and asked, "Are you Butterfly McQueen?" She smiled and answered, "Yes, I am. What are you having?" I told her that I thought I'd have banana and strawberry. She beamed and said, "I think I'll have the same." She then asked, "Are you an actor? You look like an actor." I told her yes and that I just came from a performance. "What are you in?" I told her and she said, "I'm doing *Curley McDimple*—just finished." I took the opportunity to pump her some questions. "What was your favorite movie?" She thought for a second and said, "Well, I suppose it's *Gone With the Wind* because I loved working with Mr. Gable and Miss Leigh. But I loved working with Miss Crawford in *Mildred Pierce* and with Jennifer Jones in *Duel in the Sun*." She was very charming. A few years later, when my cousin visited me here in NYC, we went out sight-seeing one day and ended up on a bus in Harlem. On the way back downtown, my cousin said, "Look back there. That lady looks exactly like Butterfly McQueen!" I looked and it was, indeed, Butterfly, who was reading a book, which was upside down. She was pretending to read the book, but was really looking around to see who was recognizing her (since there were a lot of tourists on the bus). My cousin and I thought that was very funny.[19]

Basking in the success of her "comeback" in *Curley McDimple*, in August 1969 Butterfly returned to the Bert Wheeler Theatre for an appearance in a revue called *Butterfly McQueen and Friends*, and on October 16, 1969, after an absence of thirty years from the Broadway stage, she opened at the Lyceum as the elevator operator Dora Lee in a revival of John Cecil Holm and George Abbott's 1935 play *Three Men on a Horse*. Unsurprisingly, this production was directed by Abbott, who, in the 1930s, had opened doors for Butterfly on Broadway that led her to *Gone With the Wind*. A few months later, on February 2, 1970, at the Ethel Barrymore Theatre, she replaced Dody Goodman in the role of Jennie in a Broadway revival of Ben Hecht and Charles MacArthur's 1928 production *The Front Page*.

Butterfly also made a Hollywood comeback, after an absence of twenty-two years, in *The Phynx* (1970). In this comedy spoof, a rock-and-roll band made up of U.S. agents, called The Phynx, is sent to Albania to rescue a group of kidnapped American celebrities who are being held in a remote castle by communist enemies of the United States. The hostages provided cameo roles for around thirty guest stars, mostly from the Golden Age of Hollywood, including Butterfly, Busby Berkeley, Ruby Keeler, Xavier Cugat, Maureen O'Sullivan, Johnny Weissmuller, Dorothy Lamour, and Rudy Vallee. Some of the other cameos were taken by Joe Louis, Ed Sullivan, and Richard Pryor. Intended as a major release by a major studio (Warner Brothers), *The Phynx* was barely—if ever—released and would undoubtedly rate highly in worst-film lists. Clive Hirschhorn describes *The Phynx* in *The Warner Bros. Story* as "an acute embarrassment to all concerned and, after a brief airing, [it] was consigned to the shelf."[20]

In 1970 Butterfly began working at the Mount Morris Park Recreation Center in New York. She was employed as the receptionist at the front door of the center, where she answered questions, gave directions, and sometimes corrected grammar! She also helped out as a playground assistant and gave tap dance or ballroom lessons, or guitar and piano, even French and Spanish: "As long as it's beginners," she told Charlayne Hunter in an interview in the *New York Times* (July 28, 1970):

> Her new job, after a lull in her career, evolves out of a commitment to "work with the black family." "My theme is to know that it's going to be a long time before people in general are nice to each other because families are not nice to each other," she said. Miss McQueen has many friends and two cats, but she has no close relatives. She lives alone in a brownstone rooming house she owns. In April, she said, one of the tenants threw lye in her face, but all but a small dark trace of the damage is gone. "By the time the police got there, I was sitting on top of her," she recalled. "And if I hadn't been a Christian and realized that the woman was just sick, I probably would have bashed her head into the floor. But the policemen treated us both like dirt. I don't like our police being called pigs. But some are hateful." She feels that this is a good example of why the black family must work together, which would mean, among other things, more black policemen in black neighborhoods. . . . "When I was working in a downtown show once, the star called me an unprintable word, and I took it to Actors Equity. The whole thing took so long that his girl friend called me a nigger. Thirty years ago I wouldn't have been surprised. Now, since I'm still going to be called things, let me stay up in Harlem." She says she is primarily interested in developing avenues within the black community "that keep us from always going downtown with our hats in our hands." She said more black writers and producers in television and on radio and on the stage and screen were needed "so that we can do for ourselves."[21]

In 1971 Butterfly took part in a television discussion program for NET called *Free Time* with host Julius Lester and the African American directors Ossie Davis, Gordon Parks, and Melvin Van Peebles. Said *Variety* (November 24, 1971): "Miss McQueen hit all the emotional bases as she discussed her Hollywood career and her reaction to current film trends, providing a very moving, and all-too-brief appearance. . . . Regarding the new black films, Miss McQueen enjoyed *The Learning Tree* [directed by Gordon Parks] but has avoided the others because of 'vulgar language.' As for any future roles: 'I'd like to play just an American, they can see I'm black.'" On August 11, 1973, Butterfly appeared at the Alice Tully Hall in a concert called *Soul at the Center*, and in 1974 she made another movie.

Amazing Grace was intended as a starring vehicle for the comedienne Jackie "Moms" Mabley, who had previously appeared in *Swingin' the Dream* (see chapter 5) and *Killer Diller*. Moms was one of the most successful entertainers of black vaudeville, also known as the Chitlin' Circuit. Affectionately known as "The Funniest Woman in the World," she took her stage name from a boyfriend, Jackie Mabley. In the 1970s she told *Ebony* magazine that he'd taken so much from her, it was the least she could do to take his name. Later she became known as "Moms" because she was indeed "Mom" to many other comedians on the circuit in the 1950s and 1960s. At the peak of her long career, which spanned five decades, she was earning around $10,000 a week at Harlem's famous Apollo Theatre. In her popular comedy act, Mabley focused on conventional topics, such as family, and subjects that were taboo and rarely touched upon by comedians of her era, white or black, such as infidelity, poverty, welfare, and inebriation. Mabley's unorthodox, self-assured routines made her a firm favorite with black female audiences, but her film appearances were rare. *Amazing Grace* was directed by Stan Lathan, who later recalled that he put the film together with his partner at the time, the African American writer/producer Matt Robinson:

> Matt is an expert on the history of Black entertainment. He had this idea to make a movie with Moms Mabley. It was a tribute to early Black film stars who by this time in the seventies had been mostly forgotten and overlooked by the contemporary generation. We did this little comedy for $750,000. We had to stop production while Moms had a pacemaker put in. She came back to finish the film; it was amazing. It was a cute little movie that I enjoyed making. It was my introduction to comedic and dramatic feature filmmaking. I learned a lot on the production, in terms of understanding the filmmaking process.[22]

Moms played Grace, a lovable but cantankerous widow and grandma who has a mouth that could take on the devil himself. When she learns that her neighbor, mayoral candidate Welton J. Waters (Moses Gunn), is nothing more than a white man's pawn, she takes him under her wing, and hits the streets as his campaign manager! *The Hollywood Reporter* (July 12, 1974) describes Moms as "a mumbler of the Marlon Brando school" and "an irrepressible, non-stop personality who will again delight black audiences (as she has been doing for many years) but will also be an eye-opener for general audiences as well. After a rambling beginning, *Amazing Grace* snaps sharply into focus as it gets into the nitty-gritty of its story." Butterfly shows up briefly in a hilarious cameo role as Grace's friend Clarice. A camp creation, she answers Grace's telephone call with a pink telephone. Grace, unable to tolerate Clarice's high pitched voice, exclaims: "I'm gonna get a pair of pliers and fix this woman's voice." In their brief conversation, Moms and Butterfly are very funny, with their contrasting comedy styles. Butterfly's all-too-brief appearance is a delight and demonstrates that, in the right kind of movie, and in the right kind of part, she could be a clever and entrancing comedienne. As for Moms, *Amazing Grace* was her swan song. She died in 1975.

In 1974 Butterfly was interviewed by Tinkerbelle in the November issue of the magazine *Andy Warhol's Interview*, published by the pop artist Andy Warhol. Butterfly's offbeat interview is hugely entertaining. Here is an extract:

> TINKERBELLE: The other day someone asked me to ask you if . . .
>
> BUTTERFLY: Wait a minute, wait a minute (primps and preens for Lorey Sebastian, who is snapping pictures) like this, Miss Photographer? What did you say dear?
>
> TINKERBELLE: Um, I was saying that this friend of mine asked me to ask you if you were related to Steve McQueen.
>
> BUTTERFLY: Oh! Tee, hee, hee, hee, hee, hee, hee, hee, hee.
>
> TINKERBELLE: Do you know how many languages *Gone With the Wind* was dubbed in? I imagine it would be great to see it in Japanese.
>
> BUTTERFLY: No, but people have told me that in Spain I had a very deep voice.
>
> TINKERBELLE: When you finished that movie, did you feel like you had actually lived through the Civil War?
>
> BUTTERFLY: Oh no, ah hahahahahahaha.[23]

In 1975, Butterfly was inducted into America's Black Filmmakers Hall of Fame. Others honored that year included Eddie "Rochester" Anderson, Ruby Dee, Duke Ellington, the late Lorraine Hansberry, Lena Horne, the late Hall Johnson, Quincy Jones, Eartha Kitt, the late Hattie McDaniel, and Sidney Poitier.

Around the time Butterfly returned to the screen in *Amazing Grace*, she was involved in a couple of stage productions. In 1974, in Kansas City's Waldo Astoria Dinner Theater, she appeared in the musical *Purlie* with blues singer Roy Roberts, and later that year she was in the original cast of the musical *The Wiz* when it opened at the Mechanic Theater in Baltimore, Maryland, on October 21. Butterfly played "The Queen of the Field Mice" and received fine reviews, but she left the production before it reached Broadway. In *Andy Warhol's Interview* she gave some insight into her reason for leaving the cast: "The business is very nerve-wracking. That's why I don't think I'll be able to stay in this show. I'm abnormally sensitive and see this rash? It just breaks out because oh, I get so nervous. *The Wiz* opens in December on Broadway. It's a wonderful show and they don't need me. They don't need any names. . . . I have to have peace and harmony. I cannot work in disharmony. I bloom in sunshine."[24] However, according to the Internet Broadway Database, Butterfly is listed in the original Broadway cast as a "standby" for the character of Addaperle, played by Clarice Taylor.[25] *The Wiz*, an all-black cast version of the MGM movie classic *The Wizard of Oz*, was a smash hit when it opened on Broadway on January 5, 1975. It went on to win seven Tony awards, including Best Original Score for Charlie Smalls, who wrote the music and lyrics, and notched up 1,672 performances, finally closing in 1979.

Throughout her life, Butterfly always tried to improve her education. "We were born to improve ourselves," she said. She first went to college in 1946 with the income she had saved from her Hollywood movies. During the next thirty years she undertook courses in areas including health foods, human body, politics, speech, theater, and anthropology at five different colleges: City College of Los Angeles, UCLA (University of California, Los Angeles), Queens College, and Southern Illinois University, and, in the 1970s, City College of New York, one of the largest divisions of the City University of New York, located on a hill overlooking Harlem. Since its founding in 1847, very few African Americans had met the academic standards required for admission to City College, but due to an open admissions policy instituted in the 1970s, minorities now make up two-thirds of the college's student body.

It was a proud day in June 1975 when Butterfly, at the age of sixty-four, graduated with a bachelor of arts degree in political science from New York's City College. The press picked up on this event, and newspapers across the country ran stories about Butterfly's achievement with headlines such as "Prissy Graduates" and "Butterfly Wins Academic Wings." In an interview at the time she commented: "Many people are congratulating me, giving me gifts, and sending me cards. But it's just another everyday occurrence to me. I see no reason for celebrating except as one lady pointed out, people are congratulating me for my perseverance. I only got the degree because of my mother who has passed away. She wanted me to be a graduate."[26] After graduating, Butterfly spent some time working with black and Hispanic schoolchildren in parts of New York City, in particular Harlem's Public School 153, where she patrolled the playground, picked up litter, and looked after the children. Her friend Charles Stumpf says:

At home in Harlem, Butterfly was an advocate of cleanliness and launched a campaign to "Prissy-up" the streets and pavements in her neighborhood. At Public School 153, a few blocks from her one-room apartment, she volunteered her services free of charge, five days a week, to tidy up the school's bleak asphalt playground. She also taught the children to use the trash cans provided, as well as teaching them how to behave at recess—no fighting, no littering, and, if she could help it, no candy or junk food. When she saw a boy or girl put some trash in a can she would reward the child with a nickel, saying, "Now, don't spend it on sugar." . . . She also volunteered her teaching abilities at the Beatrice Lewis Senior Center in Spanish Harlem, giving free instruction in English, French, Spanish, piano, guitar, ballet, and voice to its elderly members. In addition, she led a group of women, all in their 70s, in an exercise class and gave a few of the more agile ones the rudiments of karate![27]

In 1978 she wrote, produced, and starred in a bilingual one-act play called *Tribute to Mary Bethune* in Washington, D.C. Mary McLeod Bethune (1875–1955) was an African American teacher and one of the great educators of the United States. On July 8, 1978, Butterfly made her nightclub debut at the popular Reno Sweeney club at 126 West Thirteenth Street in New York. The club had been named after the character created by Ethel Merman in Cole Porter's musical *Anything Goes*. This was the trend-setting cabaret owned and operated by Lewis M. Friedman from 1972 to 1977. In those five years, Friedman presented a tremendous range of artistes. Some of them were legends; many were at the start of their careers. Says James Gavin in *Intimate Nights: The Golden Age of New York Cabaret* (1991): "The acts were anyone Friedman thought nostalgic, bizarre, or famous enough to fill the room. They included showbiz veterans (Cab Calloway, Barbara Cook, Blossom Dearie, Maxine Andrews), actresses taking a stab at club performing (Geraldine Fitzgerald, Diane Keaton, Ronee Blakley, Sally Kellerman), pop-rock singers (Janis Ian, Phoebe Snow), a handful of newcomers who won all the renown predicted for them (Peter Allen, Melissa Manchester, the Manhattan Transfer, Meatloaf), and a gallery of curiosities ranging from *Gone With the Wind*'s featured actress Butterfly McQueen to—in the words of Eliot Hubbard in the *Village Voice* (July 23, 1980)—'strippers, jugglers, transvestites.'"[28]

Interviewed on www.talkingbroadway.com by Jonathan Frank, cabaret singer Jane Olivor describes the club as "really special; it had such a patina about it. Performers would come there and hang around and drink. . . . it was like what I imagine the Algonquin was like back in the '40s."[29] In *The Advocate* (November 6, 1989), Vito Russo describes the club as "the center of the universe during the now-legendary cabaret revival of the early '70s. Everybody who was anybody either played its famous Paradise Room or sat in the audience to watch." In *The Hollywood Reporter* (November 6, 1989), Miles Beller says: "The Paradise Room let instruments and voices resonate, yet was not so daunting as to isolate those 'on stage' (a glorified platform, really) from those in the audience. Consequently the club imparted the intimacy of an archetypal *boite de nuit* without the latter's often claustrophobic smallness."

Butterfly gave further performances on July 9 and 10, and her act was almost identical to the one-woman show (*An Afternoon With Butterfly McQueen*, November 9, 1975) she had given for her friend Charles Stumpf at his "Theatre of the Nine Muses" in Hazleton, Pennsylvania. Pat O'Haire reviewed her nightclub act in the *Daily News*: "It's not an earthshaking show, by any means, but it is fun. Lots of fun. She's a totally disarming performer with a warm and friendly manner and a thoroughly delightful personality. She's not a great singer, and her act is a little too eclectic to have any sort of focus, but it is thoroughly enjoyable. And if she seems a bit unfocused at times, she's just once again being the lovable little ol' Prissy. And there's nothing wrong with that—never was."[30] When Butterfly returned to Reno Sweeney for a second engagement for one week from August 15, Carol Flake gave a detailed description of her act in her review in the *Village Voice* (August 28, 1978):

> She arrived on stage late and nervous, her small, plump body swathed in gauzy pastel. Her entrance was like one of those vaudeville gags where the reluctant minstrel, pushed on stage, shoots a quick scared glance at the audience and firms a tremulous amateur's smile into the cheery mask of the pro. With no introduction, she marched stalwartly into "Alexander's Ragtime Band" and "The Sunshine of Your Smile," her demure vibrato reminiscent of Rose "the Chi Chi Girl" Murphy. Her deliberate diction suggested a princess slumming it. By then, her darting glances at the audience were lengthening into tenuous rapport. She struck a firm hand-clasped pose and began to recite a passage from *A Midsummer Night's Dream*, her voice lilting in flightly musical precision. . . . After cantering through Kipling's "If" like a declamatory exercise, she slowed the pace for an arms-akimbo dialect poem called "Angelina Johnson." Butterfly learned a long time ago that white people think dialect is funny; it became her "gimmick," as she calls it. When she was growing up in Augusta, Georgia, her mother, a domestic, was strict about her daughter's speech, never allowing her to "whine," but she liked to imitate the shrill or melodic voices she heard on the street. . . . With a chance now to ham it up onstage at a campy supper club, her dormant musical comedy instincts began to revive during a medley of abbreviated old standards. Bert Williams's "Nobody" required a quick change into tattered tuxedo jacket and old Sunday hat. Her sly, understated style seemed more British stage whimsy than nightclub hotcha, particularly in

Gracie Fields's "I Never Cried So Much in All My Life." After "Tico Tico," sung in Portuguese, Carmen Miranda style, came what Butterfly announced as the "yatata-yatata" question-and-answer period. When few questions were forthcoming, her replies extended into a fragmented autobiographical monologue, touching on Ethel Waters' vulgarity during the filming of *Cabin in the Sky*; the big parties that reduced Hattie McDaniel to poverty; and her own lawsuit against a magazine that quoted her as saying she wanted to be in an x-rated movie. . . . Butterfly's voice began to rise out of control as she continued, glaring at the mostly male audience. "I believe I have earned the right to be the way I am. I believe my ancestors have earned it for me." The mask slipped back into place as she leaned coyly against the piano and mused: "If I had an opportunity, I would have a big hall and dress elegantly and sing like this, 'tra-la-la-la-la.'"[31]

After appearing at the Reno Sweeney club, Butterfly continued to perform her cabaret act, or "one-woman show," on and off for over a decade in various parts of the United States. On September 9, 1978, she made a rare television appearance, this time in a starring role in an *ABC Weekend Special* for children called *The Seven Wishes of Joanna Peabody*. Butterfly played Aunt Thelma, a wise and whimsical fairy godmother character in charge of granting seven wishes to Joanna Peabody (Star-Shemah Bobatoon), an underprivileged girl in Harlem. Butterfly played Aunt Thelma again in a sequel, an *ABC Afterschool Special* called *The Seven Wishes of a Rich Kid*, shown on May 9, 1979. It was this performance that earned her an Emmy in the category of Outstanding Achievement in Children's Programming. Butterfly's award, presented for the year 1979–1980, was the fifth Emmy to be given to a black actress. Previous winners were Gail Fisher, Cicely Tyson, Olivia Cole, and Esther Rolle.

On September 14, 1979, Butterfly commenced an eighty-eight-city tour of the musical classic *Show Boat* playing Queenie, the role made famous by Hattie McDaniel in the 1936 Hollywood movie. Her appearance in *Show Boat* was greeted with cheers and applause at every performance. On February 5, 1980, Butterfly and *Show Boat* came to her former hometown of Augusta, Georgia, and the city proclaimed the date "Butterfly McQueen Day." She later recalled: "They gave me a big bouquet and then read one of those 'Whereas . . . whereas . . . whereas' things. It was wonderful! I told them how, when my mommy was born there on Calhoun Street in the 1880s, white and blacks lived side by side and then when Georgia youths wanted to improve themselves, they moved to Florida—like my mommy did."[32] When *Show Boat* moved on to Atlanta for a three-day run, a critic gave her the following glowing review: "Butterfly received a tumultuous ovation at her entrance, literally stopping the show. When she broke into a brisk dance, it was one of the highlights of the evening. Whenever she is on stage, even in the background, it is impossible to watch anyone else. Miss McQueen remains one of the most enchanting elfin spirits of our time. In her soul, she seems to be dancing to merry music from a piper only she can hear."[33]

In 1980 Butterfly made news when she filed a civil suit against Greyhound Bus Lines and the International Security Corporation of Arlington, Virginia. On April 7, 1979, she was in the ladies' lounge of the Greyhound terminal in Washington, D.C., waiting for a bus to Tampa, Florida, when security guards falsely accused her of being a pickpocket and a vagrant. According to an article in the *New York Times* (January 10, 1980) entitled "Wounded Butterfly":

> Two security guards accused her of being a "clipper," or pickpocket. She said that when she refused to show them her bus ticket unless they showed her their badges, the guards threw her to the floor and held her until the police arrived. "Three officers showed up," she said. "They recognized me right away and told me they were my fans and that I was not going to be arrested." Even though she wasn't arrested, Miss McQueen's suit said, she suffered "physical and mental distress and agony as well as injury to her good name and reputation." She seeks $300,000 in damages.

In a Washington court, the guards, who were not named as defendants, claimed that Butterfly attacked them with a pencil. Butterfly told the court that the guards "had no probable cause" to suspect that she had committed a crime. Her lawyer said Butterfly is not eccentric, but "many times" dresses as though she is on her way to appear in *Gone With the Wind*. She said: "I don't care about the money. I just want the public to know what's going on." Though Butterfly asked for damages amounting to $300,000, she was awarded an out-of-court settlement of $60,000 in compensatory damages for physical and mental suffering (see appendix D).[34]

In January 1981, E. Graydon Carter in *Time* magazine reported that "Butterfly and her quavery drawl have now returned to Atlanta. Still a part-time playground assistant in Harlem, she will act as hostess for the *Gone With the Wind* Museum for the next four months. Then, who knows? After all, tomorrow is another day."

In 2002, Joan Jewett published *When the Rainbow Bends*, a "mother's memoir" about her love for her only child, who was gay and died in 1994, at the age of forty, from complications of AIDS. Joan reveals that it was her son, Drew Jewett, who had wanted to cast Butterfly in the PBS television miniseries *The Adventures of Huckleberry Finn* (1986). He is officially credited as the Story Editor on this production. Joan recalls:

In January 1983, Drew was promoted to Assistant/Associate Producer at the Great Amwell Company, located on Madison Avenue in New York. Later that year they began production on the Mark Twain classic, *The Adventures of Huckleberry Finn*, a four-part television miniseries, produced for PBS and its sister stations in Europe. It was a tremendously exciting project for Drew. He was assistant casting director and wanted Butterfly McQueen to play the part of the blind woman. He searched throughout the country and was elated to find her living in Harlem. She accepted that role and the script was rewritten for her part. He accompanied her to Kentucky for the filming and said she was a delight to work with.[35]

In June 1986 Butterfly took part in a four-day lecture series entitled "From Harlem to Hollywood" at the famous Apollo Theatre on West 125th Street. Others taking part in the series were Ossie Davis, Ruby Dee, Geoffrey Holder, Eartha Kitt, the Nicholas Brothers, and Paul Winfield. Butterfly, with her unmistakable voice, received the event's loudest ovation.

In 1986 Butterfly agreed to take part in the celebration of the fiftieth anniversary of the publication of Margaret Mitchell's novel *Gone With the Wind*. Officially published on June 30, 1936, the half-century celebration closed on June 30, 1986, with the issuance of the Margaret Mitchell postage stamp at Atlanta's Omni-International Hotel. Butterfly was one of the guests, and stole the show. She received the biggest ovation at the ceremony, and was the only guest to get the audience on its feet. Journalist Robert Rosterman was also in attendance, and reported to Ken Sephton in London:

> Perhaps overwhelmed by the applause, Butterfly blurted out her famous line, "I don't know nothin' 'bout birthin' babies." Perhaps such levity was inappropriate at such a dignified occasion but Miss McQueen's good humor won over the large crowd. After the speeches the guests were seated to sign First Day Covers and autographs for the audience. It was "Prissy" who drew the most attention. Fans lined up for well over two hours to receive her signature—a testimony to her memorable performance and the fondness she holds in the hearts of all GWTW fans. Today Miss McQueen is given to dismissing Prissy as "a silly part. They needed comedy relief after all the drama and tragedy." But she also realizes the importance of the role: "If Margaret Mitchell hadn't written the book and David O. Selznick hadn't made the movie, who would ever have heard of Butterfly McQueen?"[36]

In 1986, after an absence of twelve years, Butterfly returned to the big screen in her final film, *The Mosquito Coast*, starring Harrison Ford. Peter Weir directed the eagerly awaited adaptation of Paul Theroux's masterly 1982 best-selling novel, but the film received mixed reviews. But, as Don

Atyeo notes in the London listings magazine *Time Out* (February 4–11, 1987), "given that Theroux's harrowing tale of jungle craziness is one of the least filmable properties of recent years, Weir's river journey to the heart of darkness works considerably better than one might expect . . . a brave and serious piece of film-making, and if it ultimately fails, it does so with considerable honour." In spite of critical indifference, *The Mosquito Coast* contains one of Harrison Ford's best performances. He brilliantly portrays the mental decline and fall of Allie Fox, an idealistic inventor who drags his wife and children to the jungles of Central America in a doomed effort to bring ice to the natives. Helen Mirren and River Phoenix give strong support as his wife and son.

Butterfly makes a couple of appearances as Ma Kennywick, a citizen of Geronimo, the small town in the jungle where Allie Fox and his family settle, but if you blink, you miss her. Looking older and more distinguished than in her previous film appearance in 1974 (*Amazing Grace*), Butterfly has little to do other than look awkward when the Bible-thumping Reverend Spellgood (Andre Gregory) berates her for not attending church. For one brief moment, in longshot, Helen Mirren can be seen approaching Ma Kennywick and saying a few words to her. Nothing has come to light regarding the reason for casting Butterfly in the film. One can only assume that, as a well-known citizen of one of the film's locations (Georgia), her name may have been mentioned to Peter Weir, or some other person involved in the production, and she was offered a cameo role. Butterfly did make one revealing comment on *The Mosquito Coast*: "Peter Weir told me to make up my own dialogue but I did it so well he cut it out of the film."

Fifty years after *Gone With the Wind*, Butterfly made her final screen appearance—on television—as Miss Priss in *Polly*, a hugely enjoyable *Magical World of Disney* production, shown on November 12, 1989. In this musical adaptation of Eleanor H. Porter's children's classic *Pollyanna*, set in the 1950s, an orphan tries to use gladness to unite the people in a small Southern town. Child star Keshia Knight Pulliam, famous as Rudy Huxtable in television's long-running *The Cosby Show* (1984–1992), was cast as Polly, and she led a cast of familiar African American television stars that included Phylicia Rashad and Dorian Harewood. *Polly* was directed by the choreographer Debbie Allen, best-known for her roles in the film and television series *Fame*, and she does a good job as both director and choreographer. In fact, Allen received an Emmy nomination for her choreography. Regrettably, William Blinn's script offers no lines for poor Butterfly, who is nothing more than a glorified extra. She can be glimpsed in the crowd of townsfolk watching Keshia Knight Pulliam sing and dance in the enchanting "Sweet Little

Angel Eyes" production number, but if you blink, you miss her. Elsewhere in *Polly* she can be glimpsed playing the organ in the church sequence, but she deserved better. Though her earlier television role in the *Huckleberry Finn* miniseries was also minuscule, at least they gave her some lines!

Ironically, it would take her most controversial screen role, Prissy in *Gone With the Wind*, to bring Butterfly back into the limelight during the film's fiftieth-anniversary celebrations in 1989. Olivia de Havilland, the only surviving major star of the film, declined to participate. This enabled other surviving cast members to take centre stage. And it was seventy-eight-year-old Butterfly who attracted the greatest media attention with a string of personal appearances.

Notes

1. Sarah Gristwood, "Butterfly in the Wind," *The Guardian*, August 21, 1989.

2. Mel Watkins, *On the Real Side: A History of African American Comedy from Slavery to Chris Rock*, rev. ed. (New York: Simon and Schuster, 1999), 358.

3. *Beulah* (ABC), undated episode from 1950.

4. Tinkerbelle, "McQueen for a Day," *Andy Warhol's Interview* 4, no. 11 (November 1974), 19.

5. Charles Stumpf, "Remembering Butterfly McQueen," *Films of the Golden Age* (Spring 1996), 53.

6. Donald Bogle, *Prime Time Blues: African Americans on Network Television* (New York: Farrar, Straus and Giroux, 2001), 23–25.

7. Ossie Davis and Ruby Dee, *With Ossie and Ruby: In This Life Together* (New York: HarperCollins, 1998), 179.

8. Richard Grupenhoff, *The Black Valentino: The Stage and Screen Career of Lorenzo Tucker* (Metuchen, N.J., and London: Scarecrow Press, 1988), 133.

9. Grupenhoff, *Black Valentino*, 135.

10. William Hughes, *Snapshots of a Faded Past* (Philadelphia: Xlibris, 2000), 23.

11. "*Gone With the Wind* Maid Asks Help in Getting Job,'" *The New York Times*, January 10, 1966, 17.

12. *The New York Times* review quoted in the sleeve notes for the 1994 CD reissue of *The Athenian Touch*.

13. *The New Yorker* review quoted in the sleeve notes for the 1994 CD reissue of *The Athenian Touch*.

14. *N.Y. World-Telegram* review quoted in the sleeve notes for the 1994 CD reissue of *The Athenian Touch*.

15. Wendell C. Stone, *Caffe Cino: The Birthplace of Off-Off-Broadway* (Southern Illinois University, 2005), 30.

16. Guy Flatley, "Butterfly's Back in Town," *The New York Times*, July 21, 1968, D18.

17. Jane Stuart, by e-mail, May 1, 2007.

18. Mal Vincent, "Here's to a Beloved Butterfly Who's Gone with the Wind" (obituary), *The Virginian-Pilot*, December 31, 1995, 7.

19. "The Night I Met Butterfly McQueen," August 12, 2006, message posted by "nneprevilo" on Butterfly McQueen message board on Internet Movie Database, www.imdb.com (accessed February 27, 2007).

20. Clive Hirschhorn, *The Warner Bros. Story* (London: Octopus, 1979), 394.

21. Charlayne Hunter, "*Butterfly McQueen Has a Family Now,*" *The New York Times*, July 28, 1970, 20.

22. Spencer Moon, *Reel Black Talk: A Source Book of 50 American Filmmakers* (Westport, Conn.: Greenwood Press, 1997), 218.

23. Tinkerbelle, "McQueen for a Day," 18.

24. Tinkerbelle, "McQueen for a Day," 19.

25. Internet Broadway Database, www.ibdb.com (accessed January 5, 2007).

26. Stumpf, "Remembering," 55.

27. Stumpf, "Remembering," 58.

28. James Gavin, *Intimate Nights: The Golden Age of New York Cabaret* (New York: Grove Weidenfeld, 1991), 304–5.

29. Jane Olivor interviewed by Jonathan Frank, www.talkingbroadway.com (accessed December 21, 2006).

30. Pat O'Haire, "The Prissy Who Persists," *Daily News*, July 11, 1978, 45.

31. Carol Flake, "Prissy Comes Back," *Village Voice*, August 28, 1978, 109.

32. Stumpf, "Remembering," 57.

33. Stumpf, "Remembering," 57.

34. See "Poor Butterfly," *New York News*, January 10, 1980, and "Butterfly Sues: I'm No Pickpocket," *London Evening Standard*, March 26, 1982.

35. Joan Jewett, *When the Rainbow Bends: A Mother's Memoir* (Philadelphia: Xlibris, 2002), 117.

36. Notes by Robert Rosterman sent to Ken Sephton in London.

CHAPTER TEN

~

The Fiftieth Anniversary of
Gone With the Wind

The first time I saw *Gone With the Wind* I thought they should bury it, now I meet nice people and I have money.

—Butterfly McQueen, *Wogan*, BBC TV

On October 5, 1988, Butterfly was seen on American television in the documentary *The Making of a Legend: "Gone With the Wind"* (see chapter 2). The documentary is now available in the 2004 Turner Entertainment DVD release of *Gone With the Wind*. In 1989 the documentary was screened at various film festivals, and these events were timed to coincide with the fiftieth-anniversary rerelease of the film. Apart from Butterfly, interviewees in the documentary also included other surviving cast members, such as Evelyn Keyes and Ann Rutherford, who played Scarlett O'Hara's sisters. At first, Butterfly was reluctant to take part in the documentary. David Thomson, who wrote the screenplay and later published *Showman: The Life of David O. Selznick* (1993), explains how he and one of the documentary's producers, L. Jeffrey Selznick, persuaded her:

It was a strange event—some time in the late '80s. I was researching the book and the documentary with Jeffrey Selznick (one of David Selznick's sons) and we had some difficulty getting Butterfly to respond. Then she did, gave a phone number, and we arranged to meet her—at a crossroads just south of Harlem on a hot summer day. We expected to go to her place, or to a hotel, or a restaurant to do the interview. Well, there she was, but she said no, let's talk on the street. So we moved to a kind of island in the middle of the street, sat down there on a stone wall and did the interview. I suppose she was shy or afraid of going anywhere else. Well, considering the circumstances, it was a good interview—and later on, Butterfly was properly filmed for the documentary. But the most beautiful thing happened. Because of where we were, many people were passing close by all the time we were talking. But the crowd was often too dense to see anything clearly. Well, all of a sudden a young white woman crossing the street cried out, "Gone With the Wind!" She had heard Butterfly's voice, without seeing her, and made the connection. And this young woman went down on her knees before Butterfly to thank her for the film. It was very touching and entirely natural.[1]

In 1989 Butterfly happily agreed to take part in the fiftieth-anniversary celebrations of *Gone With the Wind*. There had been a two-year restoration program by its owners, Turner Broadcasting System, and the new color-corrected print, struck from the original negatives, costing $250,000, had its premiere on January 30, 1989, at New York's Radio City Music Hall. At the music hall premiere, cosponsored by the Museum of Modern Art, the screening was introduced by Butterfly, one of the few remaining actors from the film. In *The Hollywood Reporter* (February 16, 1989), Robert Osborne said Butterfly made a brief appearance on the Music Hall stage, "sweetly giving thanks to David O. Selznick," then proceeding to sing a brief ditty to the tune of Max Steiner's "Tara's Theme" with more lyrics of gratitude: "It was a preamble that raised the roof." Interviewed by Max Alexander in the *New York Times* (January 29, 1989), Butterfly remembered "Mr." Selznick as "a hard worker and an excellent person; that's why the movie is so excellent." She added that the only time the director Victor Fleming scolded her "was when I was sitting in the back of the wagon and we had to pretend that we were going through the fire—which we never saw—and he said to me, 'Ham it up, Prissy! Ham it up! You're not hammy enough!'"[2] The refurbished film was then booked into forty-one American cities, often at prestige revival houses like the Castro in San Francisco.

During the fiftieth-anniversary celebrations, Butterfly made her first trip abroad to make a personal appearance at the screening of *Gone With the Wind* in the Edinburgh Film Festival on August 20. She then traveled to London to make a guest appearance in the popular BBC television tea-time talk show, *Wogan* (August 21, 1989). It was a live transmission. Following an enthusiastic reception and loud applause, Butterfly charmed interviewer Terry Wogan and the studio audience with her memories of *Gone With the Wind* and Prissy, whom she described as "stupid and backward." Butterfly told Wogan that she tested for the part in New York, and then signed the contract, "to make money to pay for some new furniture I'd just bought." Butterfly corrected Wogan when he said the film was made very quickly: "Oh, no! He was two years searching for Scarlett, but I think that was just for publicity, and then Mr. Selznick was very painstaking and careful. It wasn't made quickly." She added that Mr. Selznick understood that no intelligent person wants to be seen as a character like Prissy: "But I did everything they asked me to, except I wouldn't let Scarlett slap me, and I wouldn't eat the watermelon which is silly. I could have ate it and spat out the seeds and sang but I was just going through a phase." The interview continued:

WOGAN: "You were being rebellious? You thought it was racist?"

BUTTERFLY: "Whatever. I didn't like to eat the watermelon."

WOGAN: "So you gave them a lot of trouble?"

BUTTERFLY: "I didn't eat it."

WOGAN: "You don't feel as strongly about those things now?"

BUTTERFLY: "No. I have studied history. You see, Mr. Wogan, my mother was tender hearted and never talked about slavery. When we were coming along, we were building America, we weren't separating different groups. We hadn't seen *Roots* or anything like that. We weren't concerned about our past, which probably is foolish. We were concerned about building the country. Now I know about slavery. I've researched history, and I know those things happened. When I was a hostess at the Stone Mountain Recreation Center, people would come from all over Georgia and tell me about things, and one man told me his grandfather had slaves and at night they put chains on their legs and put them in a hole. They did that to keep them from running away. And when the people were down there fighting about integration, I said to myself 'this is what they want to go back to?' The first time I saw *Gone With the Wind* I thought they should bury it, now I meet nice people and I have money."

WOGAN: "The film has been re-tinted and touched up, do you think it's better?"

BUTTERFLY: "It's prettier."

WOGAN: "Are you looking better in it?"

BUTTERFLY: "I think they've glamorized me a little."

WOGAN: "A little rouge on the cheeks?"

BUTTERFLY: "I think they did."

WOGAN: "You introduce the film at premieres."

BUTTERFLY: "No, I just say a few words before."

Butterfly then stood up, recited a poem, reenacted some dialogue from *Gone With the Wind*, and sang, to the tune of Max Sleiner's "Tara's Theme": "Now I must go, I hope you've enjoyed the show, it's been fun to be with you, you've been helpful too. Prissy is very silly, she's willy nilly, that's to keep you happy friend, till we are all gone with the wind." To loud applause and cheers from the audience, a delighted Wogan thanked Butterfly and said: "What a wonderful way to finish the show."[3]

When the newly restored *Gone With the Wind* was screened in Atlanta, Georgia, on Friday, December 15, 1989, exactly fifty years after its world premiere, it couldn't be shown at its original venue. The Loew's Grand, the MGM-owned theatre (or, more accurately, the theatre company that owned MGM) where the film premiered in 1939, had burned to the ground in 1977. As a result, the "re-premiere" was held at the Fabulous Fox, the sole remaining Atlanta movie palace. The Fox was one of the last and most lavish movie palaces built in America. As the name implies, it was the flagship house for Fox (later Twentieth Century Fox) in Atlanta and opened on Christmas Day 1929. It has 4,600 seats and was designed for silent as well as sound films. Says Christopher S. Connelly, who attended the 1989 "re-premiere":

Like so many larger Southern theatres, the Fox was segregated. Black patrons purchased their tickets, I believe, at a separate kiosk and climbed several flights of outdoor stairs on the Ponce de Leon side of the theatre while whites entered from the more prestigious Peachtree Street side. In the 1970s, the theatre fell into disrepair. However, after the loss of the Loew's Grand, Atlanta realized how precious the Fox was and saved it from the wrecking ball. It has been beautifully restored to its former Moorish glory and is now Atlanta's primary house to touring Broadway productions and pop concerts. Occasionally, especially in the summer, they show vintage films. Every couple of years they run *Gone With the Wind* and it always sells out. I refuse to ever watch it on television or DVD again. There is nothing like seeing the film in a beautiful theatre with an appreciative audience.

Fast forward fifty years from the original premiere in Atlanta, and we have Butterfly as the headliner at the Fox, a formerly segregated theatre. The Atlanta press soft-pedaled this in their coverage, but I am sure the irony was not lost on her. I can't remember much of her address that night, only that she was gracious, if incoherent. Then she started to sing her little song to the tune of "Tara's Theme." It was demented, but the crowd loved her. While the crowd applauded, I turned to my friend and whispered, "what an icon!" And she was. It was nice she had this final moment of triumph. In addition to Butterfly, as far as I can remember, the surviving cast members who attended were: Evelyn Keyes (Suellen), Ann Rutherford (Carreen), Fred Crane (Brent Tarleton), Rand Brooks (Charles Hamilton) (died 2003), William Bakewell (Mounted Officer who tells Scarlett to evacuate Atlanta) (died 1993), and three others who played children in the film: Cammie King (Bonnie Blue Butler), Jackie Moran (Phil Meade) (died 1990), and Mickey Kuhn (Beau Wilkes).[4]

Not everyone joined in the celebrations of *Gone With the Wind*'s Atlanta revival. In 1939 Atlanta's Ebenezer Baptist Church choir, including ten-year-old Martin Luther King Jr., had taken part in the celebrations for the original premiere, but in 1989, Reverend Joseph Roberts Jr., pastor of the church, declined an invitation for the current Ebenezer choir to recreate their 1939 performance. "It's a great old classic," he told the *New York Times* (December 16, 1989), "but it is an affront to us, and I just felt that with what has happened in the civil rights movement and especially what has emanated from this church under Martin Luther King Jr., people have a different status now."

Though it attracted a great deal of media attention, and audiences, for some the reissue of *Gone With the Wind* was an embarrassment. In America, *Daily News* staff writer Lewis Beale was unimpressed with the "revival." In an article entitled "*Gone With the Wind* Can't Shed Its Racism," he compares Selznick's epic to *Triumph of the Will*, German director Leni Riefenstahl's film about the 1934 Nazi rally in Nuremberg, not only one of the world's great documentaries but a "love poem" to Adolf Hitler: "great art can make for bad politics. . . . *Gone With the Wind* is Hollywood entertainment at its slickest and most romantic, but it is also shamefully revisionist, and racist to the core. It's about time we as a nation recognize that one of America's most popular films is also one of its most disgraceful."[5] When the movie critic Colette Maude reviewed the newly restored film for the London listings magazine *Time Out*, she described it as a "fine example of cinematic storytelling and literary adaptation; exemplary artistic endeavor it ain't." She also found the portrayal of the black characters "glaringly patronising."[6]

During the fiftieth anniversary of *Gone With the Wind*, the Freedom From Religion Foundation (FFRF) honored Butterfly with its first Freethought Heroine award at its national convention in Atlanta. Butterfly, a member of FFRF since 1981, was nearly a lifelong atheist. After a poetry recitation before the audience at the convention, she sang Harold Arlen and E. Y. (Yip) Harburg's "It's Only a Paper Moon," accompanied by Dan Barker on the piano. In 1978 she told Pam Fessler in *The Record* (April 2): "People who have God don't have to be nice to you and me because they know He's going to forgive them. But I don't have anyone to forgive me, so I've got to be nice." She told Gayle White, a reporter for the *Atlanta Journal and Constitution* (October 8, 1989), after receiving her award: "As my ancestors are free from slavery, I am free from the slavery of religion." Although she was raised a Christian, Butterfly began to question the value of organized religion as a child. She told Gayle White she believed that "if we had put the energy on earth and on people that we put on mythology and on Jesus Christ, we wouldn't have any hunger or homelessness. Christianity and studying the bible has sapped our minds so we don't know anything else. They say the streets are going to be beautiful in heaven. I'm trying to make the streets beautiful here. At least, in Georgia and in New York. I live on beautiful streets. When it's clean and beautiful, I think America is heaven. And some people are hell."

Butterfly lived modestly: no car, agent, or telephone. She happily answered fan letters and requests for autographs. For many years she divided her time between homes in New York and Augusta, Georgia. Says Charles Stumpf: "Her New York neighbors had varying opinions of her. To them she was somewhat of an enigma, depending upon which of her personality traits they observed. She was alternately generous and charming, or irascible and reclusive, but always opinionated and outspoken. Butterfly McQueen was unpredictable and unique. Her private life was quiet and simple. She neither drank nor smoked, nor set foot in a nightclub—unless she was performing there, which was rare. She never married and went through periods of her life being deeply religious. . . . At other times she was an atheist."[7]

Notes

1. David Thomson, by e-mail, December 31, 2002.

2. Max Alexander, "Once More, the Old South in All Its Glory," *The New York Times*, January 29, 1989, 23.

3. Butterfly McQueen interviewed by Terry Wogan in *Wogan*, BBC1, August 21, 1989.

4. Christopher S. Connelly, by e-mail, March 28, 2007.

5. Lewis Beale, "*Gone With the Wind* Can't Shed Its Racism," *Daily News*, March 6, 1989, 21.

6. Colette Maude in *Time Out*, August 23–30, 1989, 34.

7. Charles Stumpf, "Remembering Butterfly McQueen," *Films of the Golden Age*, Spring 1996, 58.

~

Afterword

If Butterfly had made it to London for an on-stage interview (see introduction), then the perfect venue for her personal appearance would have been the National Film Theatre, located under Waterloo Bridge, by the River Thames. It was here that I presented an "illustrated talk" about Butterfly, entitled "Pride and Prejudice," on December 5, 1995. It was a free event, and for an enjoyable and relaxed evening I told her story to a fascinated, captivated audience. I included film extracts from *Gone With the Wind*, *Cabin in the Sky*, *Mildred Pierce*, and *Duel in the Sun*, as well as some "surprises," such as her wonderful recording of "A Lady of Leisure" (her *Athenian Touch* duet with Marion Marlowe) and her 1989 BBC television interview with Terry Wogan. Reva Klein wrote in *The Times Educational Supplement*:

> The story of Butterfly McQueen is the story of an actress's ambitions thwarted and talents ignored because of the deep racism in American society. Film historian, writer and broadcaster Stephen Bourne, who has researched McQueen's life along with other black actors, will be delivering the seminar and he sees the short, incomplete career of McQueen as emblematic of many other black artists. But while others became bitter and disillusioned, Butterfly re-channeled her creative energies into education and community work. . . . For Stephen Bourne, Butterfly's fascination is based on her enduring quality as a star who was never given much of a chance to shine. "I've interviewed a lot of older black actors in this country and most will have taken demeaning roles at the beginning of their careers. They would say, as Butterfly would, that they took those roles but always did them with dignity and humanity. Very

few black actors have avoided playing stereotyped roles—even today. I have admiration for her as a survivor—especially when she has had the odds stacked against her."[1]

Two weeks later, while preparing to send some press clippings about the event to Butterfly, my feelings of excitement and joy at having presented a successful tribute suddenly evaporated when I heard that she had passed away. The circumstances of her death, on December 22, 1995, were horrific and deeply upsetting. With a heavy heart I agreed to write an obituary for *The Independent* newspaper. Her friend Charles Stumpf describes what happened to Butterfly:

In 1989 she gave up her New York apartment and returned to a modest one-bedroom cottage she owned in Richmond County near Augusta, Georgia. She purchased two similar rental cottages, which she rented out, giving generous rebates to low-income tenants. When a mother of five who had been in an abuse shelter wanted to live in one of the cottages, Butterfly knew the woman could not afford the rent, so in a typical gesture she smiled and said, "You're welcome, and don't worry about the rent." Her Georgia neighbors knew her simply as "Thelma" who was always smiling and happy and cleaning up her cottage, and watering the flowers she kept on the porch. At 84 years of age, she was in remarkably good health. . . . It was a cold day, and she felt a chill and decided to light one of her kerosene heaters. Well-meaning neighbors had often told her she should install central heating in her tiny one-bedroom cottage. But strong-willed Butterfly dismissed them saying, "I trust kerosene, but I don't trust gas." That day something went wrong. Possibly she spilled some kerosene, and when she attempted to light the heater, flames shot out, setting the room on fire. As she attempted to extinguish the flames, her clothing ignited. She struggled to reach the door. A neighbor, Alice Mae Young, heard her screams and rushed to her rescue. The fire had spread rapidly, but she managed to pull Butterfly through the door and ease her smoldering body onto a mat on the porch. Then she pulled her as far from the fire as she could. An ambulance was summoned, and Butterfly was rushed to Augusta Regional Medical Center suffering from second and third degree burns over 70 percent of her body. She remained coherent and was able to give her social security number and other information. She died later than night.[2]

Among the ruins of her cottage, firemen discovered six unsigned checks, each for $100, ready to be mailed to a number of charities. In her will, Butterfly left her rental homes to the tenants who lived in them, and her bank accounts were left to friends and, as she was a cat lover, to the American Society for the Prevention of Cruelty to Animals. She also left something to the Freedom From Religion Foundation (FFRF). In a final gesture of generosity, her body was left to the Medical College of Georgia. Butterfly left no plans for a memorial service. Her awards, including her Emmy, were left to the Schomburg Center for Research in Black Culture, located at the New York Public Library.

Shortly after Butterfly's death, I received the following letter from my friend Delilah Jackson in New York. In 1969 Delilah had worked with Butterfly in the off-Broadway revue *Butterfly McQueen and Friends* at the Bert Wheeler Theatre. Delilah, who is the owner of a large private collection of African American theater memorabilia, wrote movingly about her friend:

Hope your New Year is prosperous. Yesterday I went to the Lincoln Center research department. There was only one great article on Butterfly. When I looked to see who wrote it, to my surprise it was your name. Poor Butterfly. I am glad she knew you cared about her. When I worked with her in the show, there would be many of her fans waiting to get her autograph after we left the theater. When I was in her show at the Bert Wheeler Theatre, I never called her by her first name. I was impressed by her singing. She sat on the tip of the stage and sang many old songs from Broadway shows, one from a show called *Chu Chin Chow*. Butterfly said she took singing lessons from Adelaide Hall. This was when Adelaide was on Broadway in *Jamaica* [1957–1958].

She always studied dancing. I used to see her in an African dance class. In the 1950s she studied with Katherine Dunham. Singing and dancing was her life. In the senior citizen centers she would wear a leotard and tights and dance for the seniors. If one person was in the audience, she'd still do the whole show. She taught old people to dance.

I asked her to write her autobiography. She would say the show we did was her life story. I don't think she wanted to remember the early days. She told me she was abused. She said: "I've been hurt so badly." Prissy hurt her career. She told me that when she made *Cabin in the Sky* everyone was mean to her, but she was proud of who she was. When she went to Hollywood she wouldn't straighten her hair. She always wanted to be with her own people in Harlem, even though some of them were horrible to her. They called her Uncle Tom, and handkerchief head. She was lonely.

You could see Butterfly sweeping the sidewalks all over her neighborhood. She said, "I want to make Harlem beautiful again." She was very sincere about this work, from morning until late at night.

It is so sad she died the way she did. The house in Georgia had been her mother's. Butterfly loved her mother. So she kept the house. She told me she hated Georgia. I don't know why she went there. It must have been a vacation. She loved Harlem too much to leave it.

To think someone as kind as Butterfly would end like she did.[3]

Notes

1. Reva Klein, "From Butterfly to 'Mosquito,'" *The Times Educational Supplement*, December 1, 1995, 19.

2. Charles Stumpf, "Remembering Butterfly McQueen," *Films of the Golden Age*, Spring 1996, 58.

3. Delilah Jackson, letter to Stephen Bourne, December 28, 1995. Reproduced with permission.

APPENDIX A

~

Butterfly McQueen's Credits

Films

Gone With the Wind (MGM, 1939). Directed by Victor Fleming, George Cukor (uncredited), and Sam Wood (uncredited). With Clark Gable, Vivien Leigh, Leslie Howard, Olivia de Havilland, Hattie McDaniel, and Thomas Mitchell. **Butterfly McQueen as Prissy**.

The Women (MGM, 1939). Directed by George Cukor. With Norma Shearer, Joan Crawford, and Rosalind Russell. **Butterfly McQueen as Lulu**.

Affectionately Yours (Warner Brothers, 1941). Directed by Lloyd Bacon. With Merle Oberon, Dennis Morgan, Rita Hayworth, and Hattie McDaniel. **Butterfly McQueen as Butterfly**.

Cabin in the Sky (MGM, 1943). Directed by Vincente Minnelli. With Ethel Waters, Eddie "Rochester" Anderson, and Lena Horne. **Butterfly McQueen as Lily**.

I Dood It (MGM, 1943). Directed by Vincente Minnelli. With Eleanor Powell, Red Skelton, and Lena Horne. **Butterfly McQueen as Annette**.

Flame of the Barbary Coast (Republic, 1945). Directed by Joseph Kane. With John Wayne and Ann Dvorak. **Butterfly McQueen as Beulah**.

Mildred Pierce (Warner Brothers, 1945). Directed by Michael Curtiz. With Joan Crawford, Ann Blyth, Jack Carson, Eve Arden, and Zachary Scott. **Butterfly McQueen as Lottie**.

Duel in the Sun (A Selznick Production, 1946). Directed by King Vidor. With Jennifer Jones, Gregory Peck, Joseph Cotten, Lionel Barrymore, Herbert Marshall, Lillian Gish, and Walter Huston. **Butterfly McQueen as Vashti**.

Killer Diller (All American, 1948). Directed by Josh Binney. With Dusty Fletcher, the Nat "King" Cole Trio, Jackie "Moms" Mabley, the Clark Brothers, and Beverly White. **Butterfly McQueen as Butterfly**.

The Phynx (Warner Brothers–Seven Arts, 1970). Directed by Lee H. Katzin. **Butterfly McQueen as herself**.

Amazing Grace (United Artists, 1974). Directed by Stan Lathan. With Jackie "Moms" Mabley, Slappy White, Rosalind Cash, Moses Gunn, and Stepin Fetchit. **Butterfly McQueen as Clarice**.

The Mosquito Coast (Warner Brothers, 1986). Directed by Peter Weir. With Harrison Ford, Helen Mirren, and River Phoenix. **Butterfly McQueen as Ma Kennywick**.

Broadway Theatre

Brown Sugar (Biltmore Theatre, 1937) as Lucille
What a Life (Biltmore Theatre, 1938) as Mary
Swingin' the Dream (Center Theatre, 1939) as Puck
Three Men on a Horse (Lyceum Theatre, 1969) as Dora Lee
The Front Page (Ethel Barrymore Theatre, 1970) as Jennie

Off-Broadway Theatre

The World's My Oyster (Actor's Playhouse, 1956) as Queen Elizabeth Victoria
The Athenian Touch (Jan Hus, 1964) as Ora
Curley McDimple (Bert Wheeler Theatre, 1968) as Hattie

Miscellaneous Theatre and Cabaret

Butterfly McQueen and Friends (Bert Wheeler Theatre, 1969)
Purlie (Waldo Astoria, Kansas, 1974)
The Wiz (pre-Broadway, 1974) as "The Queen of the Field Mice"
Prissy in Person (Harlem, 1975)
An Afternoon With Butterfly McQueen (The Theatre of the Nine Muses, Hazleton, Pennsylvania, November 9, 1976)
Interludes (Town Hall, New York, February 4, 1976)
Hooray for Hollywood! (Hazleton, Pennsylvania, June 1978)
Tribute to Mary Bethune (Washington, D.C., 1978)
Reno Sweeney (cabaret) (New York, 1978)
Vincent's Restaurant (cabaret) (New York, 1978)
Show Boat (tour, 1979–1980) as Queenie

Television

Studio One: Give Us Our Dream (1950)
Beulah (1950–1952) as Oriole
Lux Video Theatre: Weather for Today (1951) as Mary
Night Beat (interview with Mike Wallace) (1957)
Hallmark Hall of Fame: The Green Pastures (1957)
Today Show (1968)

Mike Douglas Show (1968)
Free Time (1971)
Black Pride (1975)
ABC Weekend Special: The Seven Wishes of Joanna Peabody (1978) as Aunt Thelma
ABC Afterschool Special: The Seven Wishes of a Rich Kid (1979) as Aunt Thelma
With Ossie and Ruby (1981)
Good Morning America: Movie Blockbusters—The 15 Greatest Hits of All Time (1983)
American Playhouse: The Adventures of Huckleberry Finn (1986) as Blind negress
Our World (1987)
The Making of a Legend: Gone With the Wind (1988)
Wogan (1989)
The Magical World of Disney: Polly (1989) as Miss Priss

Radio

The Goldbergs (debut)
Jubilee (1943–1945)
The Jack Benny Program (1943–1944)
Birds Eye Open House (aka *The Dinah Shore Show*) (1944)
The Danny Kaye Show (1945–1946)
Here's to the Veterans (1946)
Harlem Hospitality (1947)

Discography

Cabin in the Sky (1943)—CD released in 1996 (Turner Entertainment Co.)
The Athenian Touch (1964)—CD released in 1994 (AEI)
Polly/Nature Fills the World With Love (1973)—reissued as bonus tracks on the CD *The Athenian Touch* in 1994 (AEI)

Awards and Tributes

1973 Rosemary Awards
1975 Black Filmmakers Hall of Fame *Note: In the second year of the Black Filmmakers Hall of Fame awards, Butterfly was inducted with, amongst others, Eddie "Rochester" Anderson, Ruby Dee, Duke Ellington, Joel Fluellen, Lorraine Hansberry (posthumous), Lena Horne, Rex Ingram (posthumous), Hall Johnson (posthumous), Quincy Jones, Robert Earl Jones, Eartha Kitt, Abbey Lincoln (Aminata Moseka), Hattie McDaniel (posthumous), Frederick O'Neal, Sidney Poitier, and Fredi Washington.*
1979–1980 Emmy Award for Outstanding Achievement in Children's Programming (for *ABC Afterschool Special: The Seven Wishes of a Rich Kid*)
1989 Freedom From Religion Foundation (FFRF) honors Butterfly with their first "Freethought Heroine" award

APPENDIX B

~

Gone With the Wind: Awards, Statistics, and Movie Lists

1939 Academy of Motion Picture Arts and Sciences' Twelfth Annual Awards

The 1939 "Oscars" were presented on February 29, 1940, at The Coconut Grove of the Ambassador Hotel in Los Angeles, and Bob Hope was master of ceremonies. "What a wonderful thing, this benefit for David Selznick," he kidded. *Gone With the Wind* set a new record with eight awards, and an additional honor, the Irving G. Thalberg Memorial Award, was presented to its producer, David O. Selznick. The winning writer, Sidney Howard, credited with sole authorship of the final script of *Gone With the Wind*, became the Academy's first posthumous winner. He had died in a Massachusetts farm accident in August 1939, while the film was still in production.

Gone With the Wind received awards in the following categories:

Best Film (the other nominees were *Dark Victory*, *Goodbye Mr. Chips*, *Love Affair*, *Mr. Smith Goes to Washington*, *Ninotchka*, *Of Mice and Men*, *Stagecoach*, *The Wizard of Oz*, and *Wuthering Heights*)
Best Director: Victor Fleming
Best Writing, Screenplay: Sidney Howard
Best Actress in a Leading Role: Vivien Leigh
Best Actress in a Supporting Role: Hattie McDaniel
Best Art Direction: Lyle Wheeler
Best Cinematography, Color: Ernest Haller and Ray Rennahan

Best Film Editing: Hal C. Kern, James E. Newcom
Irving G. Thalberg Memorial Award: David O. Selznick
Technical Achievement Award: Don Musgrave
Honorary Award: William Cameron Menzies (plaque)

Gone With the Wind received nominations in the following categories:

Best Actor: Clark Gable (lost to Robert Donat in *Goodbye Mr. Chips*)
Best Actress in a Supporting Role: Olivia de Havilland (lost to Hattie McDaniel in *Gone With the Wind*)
Best Effects, Special Effects: Jack Cosgrove (photographic), Fred Albin (sound) and Arthur Johns (sound) (lost to *The Rains Came*)
Best Music, Original Score: Max Steiner (lost to *The Wizard of Oz*)
Best Sound, Recording: Thomas T. Moulton (lost to *When Tomorrow Comes*)

Other Awards

In 1939 the New York Film Critics Circle voted to give Vivien Leigh their Best Actress award for *Gone With the Wind*, but the film lost out in the three other major categories to *Wuthering Heights* (Best Film), John Ford (Best Director, for *Stagecoach*), and James Stewart (Best Actor, for *Mr. Smith Goes to Washington*).

In the 1939 Photoplay Awards, David O. Selznick was awarded a Medal of Honor.

In 1939 the New York Times Annual Ten Best List included *Gone With the Wind*.

In 1940 the National Board of Review included *Gone With the Wind* in their list of Top Ten American Films, and Vivien Leigh (for *Gone With the Wind* and MGM's *Waterloo Bridge*) was included in their Best Acting list.

In 1989 the film was honored by the National Film Preservation Board, USA.

In 1989 the film was a winner in the People's Choice Awards, USA.

At the American box office, *Gone With the Wind* has been successfully attracting huge audiences every time it has been reissued. For example, the 1961 reissue took the film to number eight in the list of annual top money-making films in America (*The Guns of Navarone* was number one). In 1968 it went even higher—to number three—trailing *The Graduate* and *Guess Who's Coming to Dinner*, the latter starring the black superstar Sidney Poitier. When NBC screened the film on American television for the first time in two parts in November 1976, it became the most popular movie ever shown on the box.

According to figures published in the trade newspaper *Variety*, in 2001 *Gone With the Wind* failed to appear in the Top 20 Box Office Films in America. However, when the money taken by older releases was adjusted for inflation to 2001 values, a different top 20 emerged with *Gone With the Wind* in the number one position (with $1,299.4 million) followed by (number two) *Snow White and the Seven Dwarfs* (1937, $1,034.3 million) and (number three) *Star Wars* (1977, $812 million).

In 1977, to celebrate its tenth anniversary, the American Film Institute (AFI) polled its 35,000 members to select the greatest American films. It was the largest survey in the history of film studies. From this, the AFI produced a list of the fifty greatest American films. Members then voted again to produce a list of the top ten. *Gone With the Wind* was placed in the number one position, followed by (number two) *Citizen Kane* and (number three) *Casablanca*. In 1998, to celebrate one hundred years of movies, a similar exercise was carried out. Four hundred films were listed by AFI historians. Criteria used included critical recognition, popularity over time, historical significance, cultural impact, and major awards won. A panel of experts then voted for films from this list to produce a Top 100 list. *Gone With the Wind* was placed fourth, trailing (number one) *Citizen Kane*, (number two) *Casablanca*, and (number three) *The Godfather*.

~

Butterfly's "Essays" and "Booklets"

Acknowledgment is due to Butterfly McQueen for giving me permission to publish her "writings" (in a letter dated September 29, 1982).

In the 1970s Butterfly compiled several one-page "essays" and "booklets," containing personal comments and observations. She distributed copies of these to audiences at appearances she made in the 1970s and 1980s.

Reprinted here are four "essays," entitled "Miscellanea 1," "Miscellanea 2," "Miscellanea 3," and "Miscellanea 4," and one of the booklets, entitled "Uno. Students or Victims?"

Miscellanea 1

My writings are dedicated to all the "thinkers" and "doers" of the world as: my high school classmate, Mrs. Tony Sartori Weeks, a concerned Harlem observer, Mrs. Helen Testamark, Dr. Fine (Maths—Queens College), Dr. Wecker (Biology—The CCNY), and to each and every individual concerned with annual Harlem Day celebration.

Hatred is justifiable perhaps when one is an untaught child. I loathe myself if I permit my body to become too overweight, mostly because I can see the look on my mother's face as she says "goberish."

The writings of Booker T. Washington try to save one from the pit of hatred. Sometimes I almost hate myself and my mom for my inability to become accustomed to litter and squalor which is seen some places in our cities in spite of the hard work of our New York City sanitation men.

Why, I ask myself, was I raised to feel comfortable only in cleanliness and order? Why?! When so many others seem so content?

The title of my first writings (thank you Lena Horne) is not all sarcasm. It's a genuine "Thank You" for finding out some others do not consider us as highly as we've been taught to consider ourselves.

It's also a sincere "Thank You" for being shown graphically how a beautiful and prosperous person can age and wreck their face simply by calling one a "dog" in a hateful way.

During one of our wars many actors in Hollywood voluntarily taped radio shows for the armed forces overseas. One day at the Hollywood and Vine CBS radio station we were given a ten minute break from a taping session. The glamorous, talented Lena Horne, finding herself alone, unseen and un-heard by anyone but myself, looked me fully in the eye and with centuries of unleashed horridly bitter hatred called me "You dog!" Thank you, Lena Horne, for introducing me to the stark, pitiable misery of a top success.

Miscellanea 2

Actor Leon Janney took to his dressing room cot and never again acted in the show *Three Men on a Horse*, when he found out that two of the show's stars had weekly been taking home a thousand dollars of the box office in-come since the first week the show opened.

Leon hadn't heeded the advice of Kipling, "To fill the unforgiving minute with sixty seconds worth of distance run." Nor had he remembered Abe Lin-coln's counsel to hug a bad bargain. Neither had he believed Shakespeare's "Sweet are the uses of adversity."

Leon is a white adult and his childish actions surprised me, a black adult. I, too, was a bit peeved, but was fascinated at the skill with which some agents can word a contract as to "out percentage" any other agent or actor. I thought sure my agent, out of the Hartig Agency, had them (the producers) over the percentage barrel. Ha!

Too bad there had never been a "forgetful" Barry Farber in Leon's life. When I voluntarily worked with Barry Farber's political campaigners (against Bella Abzug, whom now I would like to see some day as president) I had not begun the habit of being a talk show guest unless I was advertising my own show. I was a guest on Barry's WOR radio show when he asked me to be. Did he keep his promise to announce my show dates? He did not. He signaled, "No, no" to Steve, his producer. He forgot, he said.

Another sincere WOR stalwart humanitarian (if he cares to be) also gave me a "blight man's promise." Co-authors (grave diggers) Barbara Kahn sat with me as I talked with Mr. O'Brien and as I saw unused time available I asked him (during taped commercials) when would he let Barbara Kahn speak out about the off-Broadway play, in which I was appearing for her. "Oh," he said, "later." I tried in vain. To this day, he, Jack O'Brien, the Christian, as Barry Farber, the Jew, gave me an empty promise. My belief concerning their behavior? Each is an incipient alcoholic (as our Christ was). In this alcoholic religious world in which we toil, the Barry Farbers have their conduct conditioned by Manachevitz [sic] wine and the O'Briens by stronger refreshments which permit them to *talk* one way but actually *act* another way.

Need any one wonder at the negativism of life? No, better spend time giving thanks for the positive *actors* while forgiving the insincere *talkers*. I pray now Leon Janney has also matured sufficiently to encounter the deceptive real and not take to his cot because he had mistaken it for the divine ideal.

Miscellanea 3

My landlord is a black man. He's a colored man, most likely. However, it is a custom today to say "black" meaning all of us: negroes, colored or mulattoes. Many of us are hybrids as the Puerto Ricans whose roots are American Indian, Spanish and African.

Through much suffering I discovered for myself that there is a great deal of "poor whiteness" in my black race. Alice Childress treats of this in her excellent play *The Wedding Band*. I use the word "poor" here to mean "poor" in goodwill, altruism and understanding among other qualities. Thank goodness these traits are lacking in only a few of us humans. Should one try to list the many humans of all races, colors, creeds and political preferences who are predominantly "rich" in these virtues, he would set himself an impossible task.

My landlord is also an M. D. and he didn't evict me or molest me even when I told him I do not believe in medicine. Whether he is a pure bred negro or a hybrid, he keeps our house clean and warm for a humanly reasonable rent. I hope he will some day understand why I have for years been praying for, and at last can sing the praises of a very much needed doctor—Gary Null—nutritionist.

～

Today, October 12, is a Columbus Day holiday. By chance I saw just now going up St. Nicholas Avenue a black man in a car. Bikes gleaming in beautiful sunlight was [*sic*] on the top of the car. Signs easily readable from the far sidewalk advertised a "championship bike race" at the Mount Morris (Marcus Garvey Park). Leisurely biking along the side of, and behind, the Republican-tidy car, were scrawny boys of assorted colors.

Today in October 1975 a black man charters a course for these youths to discover health, endurance and wholesome fun.

Yesterday in October 1492 a black man chartered the course for Christopher Columbus to discover America, a land of daily-returning opportunity, great attainable aspirations, and richly nourishing intellectual freedom.

Miscellanea 4

When producer George Abbott wrote three lines for me in the last scene of the last act of the high school play *What a Life* (Biltmore Theatre 1938), the theatre maid heard an actress ask in an unkind tone of voice, "Oh, why does she (Butterfly McQueen) have to be in it?"

Besides (a) starring in Mr. Abbott's *All That Glitters*, the actress had always been (b) free (c) white (d) and whatever else she wanted to be. Not only did she have (e) a movie producer for a husband, but also she had (f) lucrative business-owning parents (g) a Park Avenue apartment (h) and a Connecticut farm!

When I returned South in 1957 to study my home region and its people (as I came from the Deep South as a child), I promised myself if I found any prejudiced Southern women (white or black) I would remind myself to forgive them as they were probably "poor" and penniless: especially must I forgive them should they resent (as our New York actress had done) my three divinely-given properties of: (1) constant breathing (2) highly visible blackness and (3) unconventional habit of reasoning.

Most likely I was too busy in my usual habits of studying, working and having my curiosity quenched for the 3 or 4 "resenters" I did meet were each as materially "rich" and as inundatedly "things endowed" as the beautiful *What's My Line*, Arlene Francis.

The late Jack Benny once wrote me into a life-time contract—one of his own making. When I wanted to leave his show I just took my contract to my radio union and presto-change-o—I was free. I said I left because I was switched from occasionally playing Rochester's girlfriend to being Mary Livingstone's maid. This was the secondary reason. Primarily, I left the show because, Mr. Benny in a temper over Rochester's lateness, said he hated *all* Africans (I now laugh). He explained, trying very hard to sound hateful (I now believe there was a "mind-controller" in the room. Our friend, Long John Nebel—WMCA—would say a "brain-washer") that when he did soldier shows in North Africa, the dirt and squalor made him hate all Africans. Naïve me! Had I known then that here, too, in America, there was dirt and squalor, I could have helped by telling what Mr. Benny had said.

Mr. Benny's treatment of Rochester made him (Mr. B) greatly loved, and respected, and rightly so. Oh, for the wisdom during ones [sic] youth of age, study, experience and travel which one accumulates while maturing!

I'm sure those of us who are "litterbugs" would have mended our slovenly habits, had I had the courage to tell of Jack Benny's hatred of dirt. The fresh cool air of Jack Benny's honesty would have saved by having to clean and clear away rubbish in any place at any time—a job I utterly detest!

Eternal blessings on the Israeli tourist lady who spoke of New York City's dirt. It was great of CBS Jim Jensen to televise her observations. If ever I meet her I would tell her how very much we unselfish citizens thank her. Her candid concern for some of us pitiable Americans shows her magnanimity.

Uno. Students or Victims?

Most likely I had not been at the C. C. N. Y. [City College of New York] two or three weeks yet, and here I was "hot-footing" to Barnard College, asking to be admitted there. Yes, running again, from squalor to untidiness. The C. C. N. Y., 138th Street and Convent Avenue, was the fifth college I had attended. After making money in Margaret Mitchell's and David O. Selznick's *Gone With the Wind* I sought out in the Hollywood Library, knowledge of the body. After that, what next did I actually hunger for? Was it true a college education was "scott-free" in California? One only bought one's books? What a fool I had been not to have minded my mother and gone to college directly after finishing high school. Well, it serves me right, for being so hard-headed. Classes would be harder for me now as I had many interruptions by accumulated thoughts. Since high school there had been the Lincoln Training School for Nurses—the W. P. A. [Works Progress Administration], Broadway and now Hollywood. Off, I enrolled at C. C. L. A. [City College of Los Angeles]. Next U. C. L. A. [University of California, Los Angeles] then back to New York and Queens College where the entrance examination was the highest in America at that time.

After Mom's death, I "studied" the South for ten years.

Now Katherine Dunham phoned me in New York to join her at Southern Illinois University—in East St. Louis—another opportunity to study at a university. Next a staff member of the Theatre Guild had an idea for me to revive the Josephine Hull role in *Arsenic and Old Lace*—so back to New York. Again I found a few free hours in my day. This time I had a desire for a degree because then I could take children to Bear Mountain Park from Mount Morris Recreation Center, as a director of the brood. Also, my mother (deceased) would be pleased if I would finally graduate.

This place, the C. C. N. Y., was different—was it cleaner at Hunter? I asked someone. "Yes," but here people are very friendly. She was so right. Two little Asian "chatter boxes" chirped cheerily with me on my last day at the C. C. N. Y. How different from the aloof Chinese girl at C. C. L. A.

"Yes, you may enter Barnard," the examiner was telling me, "But we will have to make special arrangements for your attendance here, Miss McQueen." This I did not like. At the C. C. N. Y. I could enroll on a part-time basis—Barnard was a full-time four year college.

I told myself to stop running away from the unpleasantness of life.

I was only eleven blocks from the college. How convenient! A Mr. Alston Harris keeps blocks of well-cared for lawns and flowers for one to walk past on the way there. Two buses—Convent Avenue and Amsterdam Avenue brought one to the campus. Go back and make yourself "content" at C. C. N. Y. Tell yourself you were your Aunt Rachel's black-skinned sister who made her living digging on the Augusta city dumps. You would be sure to find something of value at this C. C. N. Y. Make yourself forget the beauty of California's free college. Forget Queens and Southern Illinois Universities. Hadn't you seen alcoholic Professors at C. C. L. A. and Queens? U. C. L. A.'s fastidious Robert Lees (*Mame*) weren't everywhere. Remember the stench of the moldy curtains when the theater groups worked on *Rose of the Rancho* at U. C. L. A.?

Things aren't always Helena Rubenstein magnolia and honeysuckle scented.

Put aside your squeamishness and concentrate on the degree. Don't see the grown white, skull-capped boys tearing paper to bits and throwing it in the air—don't hear the curse words—don't read the vulgarities. Never mind the drawings of men's genitalia on the walls in the girls' lavatories and stop wondering what was on the walls in the men's room. Stop trying to cover up the "_____you mindless apes, go back to Africa" with stamps from mail prize house ads. The stamps would stick over ethnic epithets on a bus, but not here on walls or doors of these lavatories. You will go crazy trying to understand "laws were made to be broken," as a student in Professor

Smith's class said. Was it necessary to completely destroy the poems Professor Drexler's friend sent to class? Poems about dog manure looking like little _____. "There is a virtue in sloppiness," said someone in Professor Savitch's class. True? Never mind the choking smoke of cigarettes, pipes and cigars. It won't hurt you to pick up the watermelon rind—it's right next to a totally empty waste paper basket. If a teacher is having withdrawal spasms, close your eyes, this class only meets three days a week. Do you want to end up as that young Jewish girl you saw at Queens College, sitting in a perfectly clean-walled lavatory in a comatose state, unable to utter a word? Hasn't she and others like her given you a hint of the planned "shockers" for which to be prepared? You'd better learn to laugh more, even falsely—mostly at your own surprise and disgust. Stop arguing with a young hate monger about the inanities in "the political experience," an assigned book wherein the author fills the end of the book with obscenities because he has no more vapid nothings with which to fill the pages. Never mind advising the Hispanic girl that if and when she does change her "image" the few restless radicals had several other vexing problems to annoy and distract her.

At my first college I met a "Jewish" girl who, as myself, was tailoring the word "God" to fit her personal beliefs, and here at my fifth college, President Marshek is decreeing that there will be no more majors for religious students. Hallelujah! Here at last is an institution where our strongest narcotic, religion, is going to be minored. At the C. C. N. Y. one had free help with one's income tax returns. Former students returned to give this service. Think on and rejoice in such facts as these, I told myself.

Seek students [SEEK is a state-funded program for economically disadvantaged and academically unprepared students] protest the taking away of funds, however, so many of them are such busy beavers they do not see the wrecking of good feelings toward all of them being done by a few opium users, turning Budenweiser Lounge into a den. Surely many have also observed that the narcotic users of Budenweiser Lounge are nearly all blacks and Hispanics. With the exception of a pretty mulatto girl who seems to be the decoy, only one other white youth was there (stoned) the day one "hopped-up" black was heart-breakingly "tripping" in the doorway of Budenweiser Lounge. Its all one can do to keep from crying at such a sight. Such a scene makes me thank goodness I'm an old-timer, born and raised in the segregated deep south. Poor fools, it isn't enough that they may be hindered by a frustrated, hateful male or female homosexual instructor, they willingly abort their own faculties.

Two integrated "pushers"—one white and one colored—were standing outside the Lounge, the day I was attracted to the noise. One could see they were observing their "guinea pigs" with calm satisfaction. To the great credit of the C. C. N. Y. they now have posters prohibiting the use of drugs on campus. They do not advertise that drugs are available to students as some colleges do.

The diligent students cannot hear my tutor, Jean Devis, complaining that many Seek students refuse to keep appointments for free tutorial help. A few slovenly students weaken the whole system for the many industrious ones.

It was unnecessary for a colored girl and youth to let themselves be the "money's paw" while disputing with faculty members about their Seek funds—using obscenities and calling their President a "liar." At this meeting I saw no white or Asian be so vulgar.

Many of the negro and colored girls dress in the latest college fashions—not casually (but clean) as I usually do. I never saw black or colored youths in pants with holes revealing their flesh as one white youth did. Somehow one knew instinctively that he and the one bare footed, stringy-haired, long-dressed "tripping" white girl was [sic] causing great sorrow and perplexity to their parents back home. One white youth in my film making class told me his mother did not want him to come to Harlem to a college. He was surprised to find only he was a beer drinker and snuff-user in that particular class. Also I knew instinctively the parents of the one black Miss I heard using profanity and those of the colored "upstart" who saw fit to say again and again, "bull____," when discussing Seek funds with faculty members, would have tried to tan their bottoms with hair brushes, in spite of their being college age. How did one know how their parents felt? One's own heart was full of pity, disappointment and bewilderment. More than once I had to remind myself not to "cancer" my body with grief for what I saw and heard; nor must I feel hatred toward the so-called integrationists who forcibly brought about these associations. One puzzle had been solved. If I had been a child again, never would I have needed to ask my mother why do some people hate us blacks? Or, why do some people hate Jews? We have been kept back and down, I believe, because some people feared they would be overcome by too great a democratic-disarray. Even Republican-tidy Jews and blacks understandably would want to keep away from their immediate domains such Democratic-disarray.

I, a disillusioned old-timer, knew that basic, decent Americanism was still the firm foundation of this present generation's "avant-gardism." Non-cancerous existence, if not living, lies in my noticing and being nourished by the dedicated business-like students who knew a good bargain when they saw one. These predominated, or else the whole campus would have been closed long ago. Most inspiring to me are the African youths. Next, most faculty members of any race, creed or color. Oh, that one were able to sit atop a twelve foot ladder and look into the unfathomable faces of the different Asian groups as they stream from north to south campus. For one who cherishes humanity, a rare treat is to sit in the front row of a class of Hispanics and enjoy several tinges and tones of complexions. I have seen at C. C. N. Y. purpleskinned Indian-looking students and pink and white kinky-haired students that could cause one to gaze spellbound—people I found as beautiful as the velvety black-skin people I sometime see in my own race, especially in Mississippi.

One semester alone at the C. C. N. Y. is needed by each and every student in order to see what nutations [sic] of humans there are in the same world. The magnet of the Asians and Hispanics one sees at the C. C. N. Y. is their inner charm, I believe. They run away from or, at least, keep apart from the frenzied hatred which some dividers seem to try to instill. Because they do I sometimes reluctantly have to think them a split hair more beguiling than my black race's beautiful colored people.

Spiritually, uplifting at the C. C. N. Y. is also the fact that with the new buildings may be revived the love of beauty and cleanliness of the college's beginnings.

It would be bad if the Seek fund is curtailed but, I know (as all old-time workers) that this is still America. True there may no longer be a Sears and Roebuck Julius Rosenwald (son of a Jewish immigrant) in every large city, he who gave over fifty million to help build schools for blacks and other exploited groups, the idealists of our American government are establishing basic grants by which worthy students may continue their institutional education. The 1975–1976 application deadline is March 15, 1976. The U. S. Office of Education has a Basic Educational Opportunity Grants Program that may help annually those who know themselves to be deserving and worthy of life's many valuable free gifts: "The U. S. government does not require repayment of such awards." (N. Y. Amsterdam News—2340 8th Avenue).

My first teacher, Mr. Goldon, at C. C. N. Y. did not answer me when I asked if the so-called "poor" weren't big-business. He did, however, encourage me to advance to graduate studies.

I switched majors every semester until I found the Romance Language Department. Still today I study and teach Spanish (which I first started at U. C. L. A. but was interrupted by Selznick's movie *Duel in the Sun*).

There are some excellent teachers at C. C. N. Y.—Emma Butler in the Music Department had great patience with my second attempt to learn Music Theory and Harmony. Dr. Ramirez of Puerto Rica was also a very patient person as were Dr. Socato of Ecuador, Mora or Chile, De La Campa of Cuba, Lurie of Greece, and others.

My daily appointment pad which I now use I learned to make in Professor Drexler's Art for Education class. Art teacher, Mrs. Rosenberg, gave me such a bitter "good bye" at Easter vacation time. It was all I could do to return to class after vacation. Good for me I did as she gave me a "B" for the course. I'm sure this pleased Mrs. McKnight and Mrs. Farmer, my first interviewers at the college. Another very patient counselor, Mrs. Lambert, in Dean O'Brien's office, cautioned me to stop trying to carry so many credits and it was a happy day when she and Mrs. Yankiver told me I was eligible for graduation in June 1975.

APPENDIX D

~

International Security Corporation of Virginia v. McQueen

Source: David A. Maxwell, *Private Security Law: Case Studies* (Burlington, Mass.: Butterworth-Heinemann, 1993), chapter 6, "Damages," pp. 185–86.

Compensatory or actual damages are the natural, necessary, and usual result of a wrongful act. Compensatory damages compensate the injured party for injury sustained and nothing more. Compensatory damages make good or replace the loss caused by the wrong or injury. In the following case, a 68-year-old woman was "karated" to the floor by two security guards. She received $60,000 in compensatory damages for physical and mental suffering. Some of the pain suffered because of the assault continued "intermittently" over four years between the time of the incident and the time of the trial.

INTERNATIONAL SECURITY CORPORATION OF VIRGINIA v. MC-QUEEN
  497 a.2d 1076 (1985)
  FERREN, Associate Judge.

In this civil action for assault and battery, the jury found for plaintiff-appellee and awarded $60,000 in compensatory damages for physical and mental suffering. Defendant appellant contends on appeal that the trial court acted improperly when, *sua sponte*, it vacated the new trial order it had entered shortly after trial and reinstated the jury verdict. Because we conclude that the trial court did not err in reversing itself, that all the issues were properly submitted to the jury, and that the jury verdict was not excessive, we affirm.

The underlying facts are essentially uncontested. On April 7, 1979, at about 11:45pm., plaintiff Butterfly McQueen, who had come to the District of Columbia to receive an award from the District of Columbia Department of Recreation, was waiting in the Greyhound bus station for a bus to Tampa, Florida. McQueen, then a 68-year-old woman, was in the ladies' lounge when two security guards employed by the defendant, International Security Corporation of Virginia (ISCV), approached and asked to see her bus ticket, apparently thinking she was a thief. McQueen refused to show the guards her ticket unless they displayed their badges and gave their names. At this point, McQueen testified, one of the guards "pushed me back into the room . . . karated me to the floor and I banged my ribs against the metal bench against the wall." McQueen elaborated: "I fell down. My left leg doubled under me, and my right leg went under. My right buttock hit the cement floor . . . and this rib hit the metal bench, banged up against the bench." The guards then detained McQueen and took her upstairs where she was questioned by the police before being released.

Other persons were present during McQueen's assault and apprehension, and she testified that she was "embarrassed" in their presence. McQueen also testified that, after the assault, she suffered from a radiating pain in her left shoulder and a swelling under her left knee. She further testified that she had never had either kind of pain before the assault, and that thereafter it had continued "intermittently" over the "four years" between the incident and trial.

Neither side presented any medical testimony at trial. McQueen, who testified that she did not consult a doctor until two or three years after the assault, explained why she did not do so earlier: "Because I'm ashamed of being ill. I don't believe in sickness . . . I didn't want to go and talk about how I was hurt."

The trial court submitted to the jury the issue of ISCV's liability and of compensatory damages for assault and battery. The jury returned a verdict in McQueen's favor and awarded her $60,000 in damages. It appears from the authorities that a jury may reasonably infer permanence of injury without supporting expert medical testimony when the effects of such injury according to the testimony of the plaintiff have persisted for a long period of time and there is no uncontradicted medical testimony that the injury is temporary.

In every personal injury case, the plaintiff carries the burden of proving not only that he or she was injured but also that the defendant's tortious conduct caused the injury. In the absence of "complicated medical questions," *Jones V. Miller*, 290 A.2d 587, the plaintiff's own testimony, without need for supporting expert medical testimony, will suffice to prove causation of injury. "No complicated medical question" arises when: (1) the injury "develops, coincidentally with, or within, a reasonable time after, the negligent act," or (2) "the causal connection is clearly apparent from the illness or injury itself and the circumstances surrounding it," or (3) "the cause of the injury relates to matters of common experience, knowledge, or observation of laymen."

Bibliography

Als, Hilton. "Mammy for the Masses." *The New Yorker* (September 26, 2005), 148–51.

Alvarez, Lizette. "Butterfly McQueen" (obituary). *The New York Times* (December 24, 1995), 23.

Ankerich, Michael Gene. "Butterfly McQueen." *Hollywood Studio Magazine* (December 1989), 28.

Aschenbrenner, Joyce. *Katherine Dunham: Dancing a Life*. Urbana and Chicago: University of Illinois Press, 2002.

Baldwin, James. *The Devil Finds Work*. London: Michael Joseph, 1976.

Barrios, Richard. *Screened Out: Playing Gay in Hollywood from Edison to Stonewall*. New York: Routledge, 2003.

Bauml Duberman, Martin. *Paul Robeson*. London: Bodley Head, 1989.

Bayer, William. *The Great Movies*. London and New York: Hamlyn, 1973.

Beale, Lewis. "'Gone With the Wind' Can't Shed Its Racism." *Daily News* (March 6, 1989), 21.

Beckford, Ruth. *Katherine Dunham: A Biography*. New York: Marcel Dekker, 1979.

Behlmer, Rudy, ed. *Memo From: David O. Selznick*. New York: Viking Press, 1972.

Bergan, Ronald. "A Maid with More in Mind" (obituary). *The Guardian* (December 27, 1995), 14.

Bogle, Donald. *Blacks in American Films and Television: An Illustrated Encyclopedia*. New York and London: Garland, 1988.

Bogle, Donald. *Bright Boulevards, Bold Dreams: The Story of Black Hollywood*. New York: One World / Ballantine Books, 2005.

Bogle, Donald. *Brown Sugar: Eighty Years of America's Black Female Superstars*. New York: Harmony Books, 1980.

Bogle, Donald. "The Defiant Ones." Interview with Lisa Jones. *Village Voice Film Special* (June 4, 1991), 67, 69, 88.

Bogle, Donald. *Dorothy Dandridge: A Biography.* New York: Amistad, 1997.

Bogle, Donald. *Prime Time Blues: African Americans on Network Television.* New York: Farrar, Straus and Giroux, 2001.

Bogle, Donald. *Toms, Coons, Mulattoes, Mammies and Bucks: An Interpretive History of Blacks in American Films.* New York: Bantam Books, 1974.

Bogle, Donald, and Rosalind Cash. "Is It Better to Be Shaft Than Uncle Tom?" *The New York Times* (August 26, 1973), D11, D16.

Bourne, Stephen. "Butterfly McQueen" (obituary). *The Independent* (December 27, 1995), 9.

Bourne, Stephen. "Butterfly McQueen: Pride and Prejudice." *The Voice* (September 1, 1984), 16.

Bourne, Stephen. "Butterfly Wings Back." *Gay Times* (August 1989), 44–46.

Bourne, Stephen. "Denying Her Place: Hattie McDaniel's Surprising Acts." In *Women and Film: A Sight and Sound Reader,* edited by Pam Cook and Philip Dodd. London: Scarlet Press, 1993.

Bourne, Stephen. *Ethel Waters: Stormy Weather.* Lanham, Md.: Scarecrow Press, 2007.

Bourne, Stephen. "Hattie McDaniel: More Than a Mammy." *The Voice* (January 14, 1984), 22.

Bourne, Stephen. "Hollywood's Robin Hood." *Films and Filming* (April 1988), 20–21.

Bourne, Stephen. "Star Equality: Hattie McDaniel and Butterfly McQueen in Hollywood." *Artrage* (Autumn 1989), 14–15.

Brown, Sterling. *Negro Poetry and Drama and the Negro in American Fiction.* New York: Atheneum, 1969.

Busch, Niven. *Duel in the Sun* (1941). London: W. H. Allen, 1947.

Cameron, Judy, and Paul J. Christman. *The Art of "Gone With the Wind": The Making of a Legend.* New York: Prentice-Hall, 1989.

Carrier, Jeffrey L. *Jennifer Jones: A Bio-Bibliography.* New York: Greenwood Press, 1990.

Clarens, Carlos. *George Cukor.* London: Secker and Warburg, 1976.

Clark, Champ. *Shuffling to Ignominy: The Tragedy of Stepin Fetchit.* New York: iUniverse, 2005.

Couri Hay, R. "Lena!" *Andy Warhol's Interview* (January 1973), 20–25.

Cripps, Thomas. *Making Movies Black: The Hollywood Message Movie from World War II to the Civil Rights Era.* New York and Oxford: Oxford University Press, 1993.

Cripps, Thomas. *Slow Fade to Black: The Negro in American Film, 1900–1942.* London, Oxford, and New York: Oxford University Press, 1977.

Cunard, Nancy, ed. *Negro: An Anthology.* New York: Frederick Ungar, 1970.

DelGaudio, Sybil. "I'd Walk a Million Miles for One of Her Smiles: The Mammy in Hollywood Film." *Jump Cut* 28 (April 1983), 23–25.

Epstein, Edward Z. *Portrait of Jennifer: A Biography of Jennifer Jones.* New York: Simon and Schuster, 1995.

Fessler, Pam. "Butterfly's Flights of Fancy." *The Record* (April 2, 1978), 21.

Flake, Carol. "Prissy Comes Back." *Village Voice* (August 28, 1978), 109.

Flamini, Roland. *Scarlett, Rhett and a Cast of Thousands: The Filming of "Gone With the Wind."* New York: Andre Deutsch, 1975.

Flatley, Guy. "Butterfly's Back in Town." *The New York Times* (July 21, 1968), 18.

Fordin, Hugh. *MGM's Greatest Musicals: The Arthur Freed Unit.* New York: Da Capo Press, 1996.

Gavin, James. *Intimate Nights: The Golden Age of New York Cabaret.* New York: Grove Weidenfeld, 1991.

Gill, Brendan. "Stories of People, Black and White, Who Fulfill Their Destinies Late in Life." *The Journal of Blacks in Higher Education* 14 (Winter 1996–1997), 137–39.

Gray, John. *Blacks in Film and Television: A Pan-African Bibliography of Films, Filmmakers, and Performers.* New York: Greenwood Press, 1990.

Green, Stanley. *Hollywood Musicals: Year by Year.* Milwaukee, Wis.: Hal Leonard, 1990.

Gristwood, Sarah. "Butterfly in the Wind." *The Guardian* (August 21, 1989), 23.

Harmetz, Aljean. *On the Road to Tara: The Making of "Gone With the Wind."* New York: Harry N. Abrams, 1996.

Harris, Warren G. *Clark Gable: A Biography.* London: Aurum Press, 2002.

Harvey, Stephen. *Directed by Vincente Minnelli.* New York: Museum of Modern Art / Harper and Row, 1989.

Harwell, Richard, ed. *"Gone With the Wind": The Screenplay by Sidney Howard.* New York: Collier Books, 1980.

Harwell, Richard, ed. *White Columns in Hollywood: Reports from the "Gone With the Wind" Sets.* Macon, Ga.: Mercer University Press, 1982.

Haver, Ronald. *David O. Selznick's Hollywood.* New York: Bonanza Books, 1980.

Herbert, Ian. *Who's Who in the Theatre.* 16th ed. London: Pitman, 1977.

Higham, Charles, and Joel Greenberg. *Hollywood in the Forties.* London: A. Zwemmer, 1968.

Hill, Errol. *Shakespeare in Sable: A History of Black Shakespearean Actors.* Amherst: University of Massachusetts Press, 1984.

Hill, George, with Chas Floyd Johnson and Lorraine Raglin. *Black Women in Television: An Illustrated History and Bibliography.* New York and London: Garland, 1990.

Hine, Darlene Clark, ed. *Facts On File Encyclopedia of Black Women in America: Theater Arts and Entertainment.* New York: Facts On File, 1997.

Horne, Lena, with Richard Schickel. *Lena.* London: Andre Deutsch, 1966.

Hughes, Langston, and Milton Meltzer. *Black Magic: A Pictorial History of the African-American in the Performing Arts.* Englewood Cliffs, N.J.: Prentice-Hall, 1967.

Hunter, Charlayne. "Butterfly Has a Family Now." *The New York Times* (July 28, 1970), 20.

Jackson, Carlton. *Hattie: The Life of Hattie McDaniel.* London: Madison Books, 1990.

Johnston, Sheila. "Back with the Wind." *The Independent* (August 25, 1989), 18.

Jones, Lisa. "The Defiant Ones: A Talk with Film Historian Donald Bogle." *Village Voice Film Special* (June 1991), 69, 88.

Katz, Ephraim. *The Macmillan Film Encyclopedia.* 4th ed. London: Macmillan, 2001.

Keyes, Evelyn. *Scarlett O'Hara's Younger Sister*. London: W. H. Allen, 1978.

Kisch, John, and Edward Mapp. *A Separate Cinema: Fifty Years of Black Cast Posters*. New York: Noonday Press, 1992.

Klein, Reva. "From Butterfly to 'Mosquito.'" *The Times Educational Supplement* (December 1, 1995), 19.

Lambert, Gavin. *On Cukor*. London and New York: W. H. Allen, 1973.

Landay, Eileen. *Black Film Stars*. New York: Drake, 1973.

Larkin, Colin. *The Guinness Who's Who of Film Musicals*. London: Guinness, 1994.

LaValley, Albert J. *Mildred Pierce*. Wisconsin/Warner Bros. Screenplay Series. Madison: University of Wisconsin Press, 1980.

Leab, Daniel J. *From Sambo to Superspade: The Black Experience in Motion Pictures*. London: Secker and Warburg, 1975.

Leff, Leonard J. *Hitchcock and Selznick: The Rich and Strange Collaboration of Alfred Hitchcock and David O. Selznick in Hollywood*. London: Weidenfeld and Nicholson, 1988.

Leff, Leonard J., and Jerold L. Simmons. *The Dame in the Kimono: Hollywood, Censorship, and the Production Code from the 1920s to the 1960s*. London: Weidenfeld and Nicholson, 1990.

Lewis, W. Arthur. "Gone With the Wind: Film Review." *League of Coloured Peoples News Letter* 9 (London) (June 1940), 50–51.

Lumet Buckley, Gail. *The Hornes: An American Family*. London: Weidenfeld and Nicholson, 1987.

Malcolm X. *The Autobiography of Malcolm X*. London: Hutchinson, 1966.

Mann, William J. "High-Hat Hattie: The Life of Movie Great Hattie McDaniel." *Frontiers* (March 17, 2000), 65–68.

Mapp, Edward. *African Americans and the Oscar: Seven Decades of Struggle and Achievement*. Lanham, Md., and Oxford: Scarecrow Press, 2003.

Mapp, Edward. *Blacks in American Films: Today and Yesterday*. Metuchen, N.J.: Scarecrow Press, 1972.

Mapp, Edward. *Directory of Blacks in the Performing Arts*. 2nd ed. London: Scarecrow Press, 1990.

McDaniel, Hattie. "What Hollywood Means to Me." *The Hollywood Reporter* (September 29, 1947), 10–11.

McDonald, J. Fred. *Blacks and White TV: Afro-Americans in Television since 1948*. Chicago: Nelson-Hall, 1983.

McGilligan, Patrick. *George Cukor: A Double Life*. London and Boston: Faber and Faber, 1991.

McVay, Douglas. *The Musical Film*. London: A. Zwemmer, 1967.

Minnelli, Vincente, with Hector Arce. *I Remember It Well*. London: Angus and Robertson, 1975.

Mitchell, Margaret. *Gone With the Wind* (1936). London: Macmillan / Pocket Papermac, 1971.

Moshier, W. Franklyn. *The Films of Jennifer Jones*. San Francisco: W. Franklyn Moshier, 1978.

Naremore, James. *The Films of Vincente Minnelli*. Cambridge: Cambridge University Press, 1993.

Newcomb, Horace, ed. *Encyclopedia of Television*. Chicago and London: Fitzroy Dearborn, 1997.

Newquist, Roy. *Conversations with Joan Crawford*. New York: Citadel, 1980.

Noble, Peter. *The Negro in Films*. London: Skelton Robinson, 1948.

Null, Gary. *Black Hollywood: The Negro in Motion Pictures*. Secaucus, N.J.: Citadel Press, 1975.

O'Haire, Pat. "The Prissy Who Persists." *Daily News* (July 11, 1978), 45.

Osborne, Robert. *Academy Awards Illustrated: A Complete History of Hollywood's Academy Awards in Words and Pictures*. La Habra, Calif.: ESE, 1969.

Osborne, Robert. *75 Years of the Oscar: The Official History of the Academy Awards*. New York and London: Abbeville Press, 2003.

Patterson, John S. "Butterfly McQueen's Lesson in Hanging On." *The Villager* (August 10, 1978), 7.

Peary, Danny. *Alternate Oscars*. London and New York: Simon and Schuster, 1993.

Peary, Danny. *Cult Movie Stars*. New York: Simon and Schuster / Fireside, 1991.

Pendreigh, Brian. "Why 'Who Dat' Became That's Enough of That, Thank You." *The Scotsman* (August 21, 1989), 16.

Peterson, Bernard L., Jr. *A Century of Musicals in Black and White: An Encyclopedia of Musical Stage Works By, About, or Involving African Americans*. Westport, Conn.: Greenwood Press, 1993.

Powers, Anne, ed. *Blacks in American Movies: A Selected Bibliography*. Metuchen, N.J.: Scarecrow Press, 1974.

Pratt, William. *Scarlett Fever: The Ultimate Pictorial Treasury of "Gone With the Wind."* London: Collier MacMillan, 1977.

Quirk, Lawrence J. *The Films of Joan Crawford*. New York: Citadel Press, 1968.

Reed, Bill. *Hot from Harlem: Profiles in Classic African-American Entertainment*. Los Angeles: Cellar Door Books, 1998.

Ripley, Alexandra. *Scarlett*. London: Macmillan, 1991.

Rosen, Paul. *High Camp: A Gay Guide to Camp and Cult Films*. Vol. 1. San Francisco, Calif.: Leyland, 1994.

Sampson, Henry T. *Blacks in Black and White: A Source Book on Black Films*. 2nd ed. London: Scarecrow Press, 1995.

Sampson, Henry T. *Blacks in Blackface: A Source Book on Early Black Musical Shows*. London: Scarecrow Press, 1980.

Sampson, Henry T. *Swingin' on the Ether Waves: A Chronological History of African Americans in Radio and Television Broadcasting, 1925–1955*. Vols. 1 and 2. Lanham, Md.: Scarecrow Press, 2005.

Shipman, David. *The Great Movie Stars: The Golden Years*. London: Hamlyn, 1970.

Shipman, David. *The Story of Cinema*. London: Hodder and Stoughton, 1982.

Simpson, Paul, ed. *The Rough Guide to Cult Movies*. London: Penguin Books, 2001.

Smith, Mona Z. *Becoming Something: The Story of Canada Lee*. New York: Faber and Faber, 2004.

Steinberg, Cobbett. *Reel Facts: The Movie Records Books*. New York: Vintage Books, 1982.

Stevens, John D. "The Black Reaction to *Gone With the Wind*." *Journal of Popular Film* 2 (Fall 1973), 366–71.

Stowe, Harriet Beecher. *Uncle Tom's Cabin* (1852). Secaucus, N.J.: Longriver Press, 1976.

Stumpf, Charles. "Remembering Butterfly McQueen." *Films of the Golden Age* (Spring 1996), 50–58.

Summers, Murray. "Butterfly McQueen Was One of the Women Too." *Filmograph* 3, no. 4 (1973), 7–8.

Taylor, Helen. *Scarlett's Women: "Gone With the Wind" and Its Female Fans*. London: Virago Press, 1989.

Thomas, Bob. *Selznick*. New York: Doubleday, 1970.

Thomson, David. *Showman: The Life of David O. Selznick*. London: André Deutsch, 1993.

Tinkerbelle. "McQueen for a Day." *Andy Warhol's Interview* 4, no. 11 (November 1974), 18–19.

Turner, Adrian. *A Celebration of "Gone With the Wind."* New York: Gallery Books, 1990.

Van Deburg, William L. *Slavery and Race in American Popular Culture*. Madison, Wis.: University of Wisconsin Press, 1984.

Vincent, Mal. "Here's to a Beloved Butterfly Who's Gone with the Wind" (obituary). *The Virginian-Pilot* (December 31, 1995), 7.

Walker, Alice. *You Can't Keep a Good Woman Down*. London: Women's Press, 1982.

Walker, John, ed. *Halliwell's Who's Who in the Movies*. 2nd ed. London: HarperCollins, 2001.

Wallace, Michele. "'I Don't Know Nothin' 'Bout Birthin' No Babies!'" *Village Voice* (December 5, 1989), 112.

Wallace, Michele. "When Dream Girls Grow Old." *Village Voice* (January 30, 1996), 21.

Warfield, Nancy D. "Gone With the Wind—1939." *The Little Film Gazette of N. D. W.* 3, no. 1 (November 1978), 33.

Waters, Ethel, with Charles Samuels. *His Eye Is on the Sparrow*. New York: Da Capo, 1992. First published London: W. H. Allen, 1951.

Watkins, Mel. *On the Real Side: A History of African American Comedy from Slavery to Chris Rock*. New York: Simon and Schuster, 1994 (revised 1999).

Watkins, Mel. *Stepin Fetchit: The Life and Times of Lincoln Perry*. New York: Pantheon Books, 2005.

Watts, Jill. *Hattie McDaniel: Black Ambition, White Hollywood*. New York: Amistad, 2005.

Williams, Linda. *Playing the Race Card: Melodramas of Black and White from Uncle Tom to O. J. Simpson*. Princeton, N.J., and Oxford: Princeton University Press, 2001.

Wilson, John S. "Butterfly McQueen Squeaks Along." *The New York Times* (July 12, 1978), 17.

Woll, Allen. *Black Musical Theatre: From Coontown to Dreamgirls*. Baton Rouge and London: Louisiana State University Press, 1989.

Index

Names

Films

Theatre

Television

Radio

~

About the Author

Stephen Bourne is the author of *Aunt Esther's Story* (1996, a biography of his aunt, a black seamstress born in London before the First World War), *Brief Encounters* (1996), *A Ship and a Prayer* (1999), *Black in the British Frame: The Black Experience in British Film and Television* (second edition, 2001), *Sophisticated Lady: A Celebration of Adelaide Hall* (2001), *Elisabeth Welch: Soft Lights and Sweet Music* (Scarecrow Press, 2005), *Speak of Me as I Am: The Black Presence in Southwark Since 1600* (2005), and *Ethel Waters: Stormy Weather* (Scarecrow Press, 2007). He has contributed to *British Historical Cinema* (2002), *Black and Asian Performance at the Theatre Museum: A User's Guide* (2003), *The Encyclopedia of British Film* (2005), *British Queer Cinema* (2006), and *The Oxford Companion to Black British History* (2007). He has coresearched *100 Black Screen Icons*, a website for Every Generation and the British Film Institute. He has organized many film and television events for the National Film Theatre in London, including retrospectives dedicated to the careers of Ethel Waters (1993), Elisabeth Welch (1994), Anna May Wong (1995), Paul Robeson (1998), and Edric Connor (1998). For British television he was a researcher on Channel 4's *Sophisticated Lady* (1989, a profile of Adelaide Hall), Channel 4's *We Sing and We Dance* (1992, a profile of the Nicholas Brothers), and BBC-2's *Black and White in Colour* (1992, a two-part history of black people in British television). For the BBC's Windrush season in 1998, he researched and scripted Radio 2's *Their Long Voyage Home*. Stephen has been interviewed in several documentaries, including Channel 4's *Black Divas* (1996), BBC-2's *Black Britain* (1997), and *Paul*

Robeson: Here I Stand (1999, an *American Masters* presentation). In 2007 Stephen was interviewed by the Criterion Collection for the documentary *True Pioneer: The British Films of Paul Robeson* in their special-edition DVD box set of Paul Robeson's films. Stephen has received two Race in the Media awards from the Commission for Racial Equality, and for *Black in the British Frame* he was short-listed for *The Voice* newspaper's Black Community Award for Literature. In 1988 Stephen graduated from the London College of Printing with a bachelor of arts honors degree in film and television, and in 2006 he was awarded a master of philosophy (MPhil) degree from De Montfort University in Leicester.